# NO MORE RAMEN

# NO MORE RAMEN

## the 20-something's
## real world survival guide

nicholas aretakis

### with 20-somethings from coast to coast

next stage press

Published by
**Next Stage Press, LLC,**
24950 N. 107th Place
Scottsdale AZ 85255
480.993.3740
www.NextStagePress.com
www.NoMoreRamenOnline.com

Editorial consultation, research, and promotion by IMS, Inc., Scottsdale, Arizona
www.IMSbreakthrough.com

Product development, management, and editing by
BookStudio, LLC, Scottsdale, Arizona

BookStudio

Cover and book design by Zuppa Design, Encinitas, California

zuppadesign

Aretakis, Nicholas.

    No more ramen : the 20-something's real world survival guide /
Nicholas Aretakis ; with 20-somethings from coast to coast. --
Scottsdale, AZ : Next Stage Press, c2006.

    p. ; cm.

    ISBN-13: 978-0-9776224-0-5
    ISBN-10: 0-9776224-0-1
    "Straight talk on jobs, money, balance, life and more."--Cover.

    Includes bibliographical references and index.

    1. Young adults--Life skills guides. 2. Young adults--Conduct of
life. 3. Young adults--Vocational guidance. 4. Young adults--
Finance, Personal. 5. Job hunting. I. Title.

HQ799.5 .A74 2006                                          2006923646
646.7/00842--dc22                                          0608

## THiS BOOK iS DEDiCATED TO

all the 20-somethings who felt they couldn't,
but learned that they could, and then
went on to affect a change.


This book is also dedicated to my first born,
Ella Nicole Aretakis, and my second baby on the way,
and any more children that may surprise us in the future.
i hope that these stories, strategies, and tips will help
you navigate through your 20s, and i hope i am
not too old to remember and help.

**ACKNOWLEDGMENTS** I'd like to thank my immediate family for their support, especially through young adulthood when I required direction. My parents' encouragement served as inspiration during my early days at college. I recall a conversation I had with them during my first semester, telling them that I was still struggling to adjust. Their simple reply was, "Do the best that you can, we're very proud of you regardless." It's not exactly eloquent, but it was all that was necessary to take off any external pressure and allow me to settle into a routine that did not satisfy anyone's ambition but my own.

To my mother, who defined commitment to family and home. She was the center of our universe and the foundation for our home. I always had confidence that she would meet our needs, no matter how challenging the situation appeared.

To my dad, an easy-going and genuinely nice guy who smiled even during the most difficult times. A World War II veteran, I thank him and many others who protected the freedom and liberty we enjoy today.

To my brother and sister, who recognized success far ahead of me and therefore were such great role models. I couldn't be prouder of either of them as they've balanced their professional and family lives so well.

To the love of my life, Ginger, my wife, who has provided me with friendship, affection, consistency, and uncompromising love. We have shared so much, and together, our lives have just begun with the birth of Ella Nicole and our second baby on the way.

I appreciate all of the bosses, subordinates, and colleagues, customers and competitors, friends and adversaries that I have interacted with over the years, for I have learned the endless lessons that I share in this book.

# CONTENTS

# iNTRODUCTiON

**TEN FOR A DOLLAR** At least that's what they used
to cost when I was in college. Of course I'm talking about ramen
noodles, the staple food of hungry students and real world
newbies everywhere. In a country where over 65 percent of
high school graduates go to college and many of those sign on
for graduate degrees, ramen noodles are not only a cash cow
for the companies that sell them but the power food that has
fueled all-nighters, long treks across campus, and many parties
for a couple of generations.

I ate ramen noodles, and so did everyone I know. When we
graduated, my friends and I may have wanted to get good jobs
and make some money, but unspoken, our goal was to be able
to afford to eat something other than those wavy noodles and
to be happy—two things we hoped life would offer post school.

For some of us the transition was easy, for others, they're still
going through it at 40. But one thing is true, when you don't

have to eat ramen anymore, you can honestly say, you have arrived. At least arrived at the beginning of a lifelong journey toward happiness in the "real world." I hope you're hungry.

Of course, I mean hungry in the figurative sense. I know I was in my 20s. I was hungry to start my career and my life and to prove to myself that I could do it. It was during a summer several years before I was out on my own that I took a job working construction—actually working a jackhammer. It was the kind of nine-to-five job that was more like six to six, and each hour left an indelible mark on every muscle in my body. To make matters worse, I was working for my girlfriend's dad. He was the owner of the construction company. I know, what was I thinking?

Well, the reality was the money was good, and when your parents are struggling to put three kids through college you take a job that can help pay the bills. Little did I know that it would also help shape my entire life with the lesson of hard work and the value of ambition. My boss, maybe because he was afraid I would marry his daughter, used to tell me, "Aim high, so this," he said as he looked around the job site, "isn't your life." Not because there's anything wrong with working construction, but just that it is a hard life. I know today that he wanted better for me. He was a tough, but caring man.

It was he, along with my father, a hardworking man in his own right, who provided me with ambition and drive. But that was over twenty years ago. What could possibly be relevant in my past experiences to the issues people in their 20s are facing today? Well, my answer is everything. Because, you see, you are in the same place I was. You possess a level of ambition—high, low, or somewhere in between—and you have your whole life ahead of you. So what do you do? That's what this book will help you decide.

Whether you realize it or not, the choices you make today will set you up for your future. And just as I chose to pursue a career in the world of technology and travel all over the world, you'll be making similar choices. Maybe for you it will be social services work in a third world country. Or maybe it will be teaching fifth grade in a small farm town or a big city. Whatever path you take, you'll learn things, you'll grow, and you'll become a different person.

Over the past year, I've talked with hundreds of people in their 20s. I sat down with them and asked them the tough questions. We videotaped all the sessions and gleaned the stories, the issues, the facts, the dreams, the fears, the passions, everything you'll find in this book. It was amazing how much alike everyone was and how similar the issues are now to the ones I faced twenty years before. The bottom line is everyone is trying to grow and learning how.

You need to know going in that growth can be tough. Emerging from the academic world to a world with no boundaries can be scary. Of course it is; as a 20-something school is much of what you know about life. But growth is necessary and natural. My hope is that I can do for you what my construction boss did for me: Provide you with direction and a path, make growth easier, and teach you a few things about life and happiness. Relax . . . no jackhammer required.

# 1

# YOU TOLD ME WHAT TO PUT iN THiS BOOK

**I'M NICHOLAS ARETAKIS AND I'VE SPENT** the last year talking with hundreds of people in their 20s all over the country. I've also spent the last twenty years living my life and helping people in their 20s make their way through what I believe is the biggest life transformation there is— going from youth to adulthood. Nobody warns you, but it happens just the same. The confusion sets in, and well, the rest is what you are feeling right now.

# 20-SOMETHiNGS.
When you do as much traveling as I did over the course of several months to find my co-authors for this book, you end up not only covering a lot of miles, but also meeting a lot of interesting people. The people I met were all in their 20s—that was part of the deal—and they were all people who said they wanted to share their stories and tell me what it's like to be 20-something in the 2000s.

Why would a guy like me want to talk with a bunch of 20-somethings, and get caught back up in the drama that I lived and made it through decades before? Why would I want to dredge up all those feelings of confusion, all those questions, all that awkwardness that comes with this time of life? Well, the reason is I had to. I had to if I was going to know for sure that the hundreds of people who I have helped along through the years were just odd ducks or typical of people going through a major transition in life. I needed to have that foundation before writing this book.

The good news is that after meeting a few hundred 20-something co-authors, I found out what I needed to know: that the people I've helped over the years weren't odd ducks at all. They were normal. And the problems and concerns that the people in Arizona had weren't all that different from the ones that the people in Kansas and L.A. had. The bottom line is that every group I met with said that this is a tough time of life and that they could use a little help. So I wrote this book to try and help as much as I can.

# THE MORE THiNGS CHANGE, THE MORE THEY STAY THE SAME.
So let's be straight with each other right up front. After all, my co-authors were honest with me, so I want to be honest with you. You'll read

some things in this book that you'll be happy about, and you'll read some things that will make you say, "Crap, does it really have to be that way?" I have to admit that what my co-authors told me often made me ask, "Is that really the way it is?" Yes, there were times when what my co-authors said surprised me. And then there were times when what they said made me remember. I would think, "Yep, I can relate," and that was mostly the case.

You see, despite what the media says, I don't think what people in their 20s are going through right now is all that different than what people in their 20s have been going through for generations. It's just that the circumstances, the environment, and the options are different. All the articles about 20-somethings make you out to be some sort of strange new sensation, like a mutant species. The writers and researchers have given you all sorts of names, like Twixters, Tweeners, and Peter Pans, not to mention Gen X-ers, Gen Y-ers, and even more derogatory terms like slackers, boomerang kids, and kidults. They've even made up names for your new stage of life, like "youthhood" and "adultescence."

I don't get it. Especially when you consider that many of these people who are either using these names or maybe even made them up (it's hard to find anyone to take credit for any of them) were likely the same people who 30 years before took off for the California coast in a desperate attempt to "find themselves" or who 20 years ago set themselves on a course to "have it all," whatever "it" was to them. A rose by any other name, as they say. We were all seeking our own form of happiness; we were all just calling it something different.

# i BET YOU CAN RELATE. Even though I am in my 40s,
I know from talking with hundreds of people in their 20s, helping hundreds more, and being 20-something myself once, that the

bottom line is you are looking for your own personal happiness. That is the way it has always been, and that is the way it will always be.

## HERE ARE A FEW OTHER THINGS YOU TOLD ME ABOUT HOW YOU ARE FEELING AT THIS STAGE IN YOUR LIFE

- You have obligations and debts hanging over you.
- Your number one priority isn't money, but you're tired of eating ramen.
- Your priority is enjoying life right now.
- You want to maintain a sense of freedom.
- You're afraid of making a mistake and not even knowing it.
- You've probably had at least a few starts and stops.
- You're hungry to get started, really started, but you're not sure how.
- You're not about to sell out your passion for a job.
- You're confused and worried about your future.
- You don't feel prepared for the real world.
- You really just want to be happy.

Welcome to adulthood. You just hinted at the life that everyone leads and the things that everyone feels at one point or another as an adult. This book addresses each and every want, need, and concern voiced in these statements, and gives some insight and advice that might be helpful to get you moving toward a happy life. These are all things I've learned from either being there or talking to a lot of people who are there now.

# BEiNG 20-SOMETHiNG
## . . . YESTERDAY AND TODAY

THE WAY YOU FEEL
IN YOUR 20s TODAY ISN'T THAT MUCH
DIFFERENT THAN IT WAS 20 YEARS AGO, BUT
THE CIRCUMSTANCES SURROUNDING YOU SURE ARE.

|  | 1980s | 2000s |
|---|---|---|
| Finding a job | Sunday paper | CraigsList |
| Create a résumé | Smith Corona electric typewriter | Laptop |
| Send a résumé | Snail mail | Email |
| Making a call | Gigantic cordless phone | Cell phone in the car |
| Required to get ahead | College degree | Advanced degree |
| Jobs in 3 years | 1 | 3 |
| Grads with loans | 1 out of 2 | 2 out of 3 |
| Years to graduate | 4 years | 5 years |
| Amount owed | $6,500 | $17,600 |
| Living | With roommate | With parents |
| Finding a date | Stairmaster at the gym | Match.com |

# 20s iN THE 80s.

It's true, when I was looking for my first real job, I looked in the want ads of the Sunday paper, and I used a Smith Corona electric typewriter and White Out. Doing multiple résumés was just that, typing up different versions on Classic Crest Linen paper—off white, so it stood out on a desk of papers. Then I folded a perfect gatefold (if the fold wasn't straight I knew I'd end up in the dud pile), stuck the letter and résumé in an envelope, licked the envelope and a stamp, sealed it, and sent it off snail mail. (Did I remember to sign it? Panic! If I didn't sign it, I was in the dud pile again.) If you were really serious you sent your résumé to a typesetter and had it professionally set in Times Roman (so much classier than typewriter Courier) and professionally printed on really nice paper.

There are a lot of differences in how I did things, but one thing is the same: I may have been in my 20s in the 80s but just like you I hungered to find my place in the world. I wanted to get started in life, whatever that life would be. I longed to figure out who I was, and what I liked and what I didn't. I wanted to find friends in new places, and just find my way around. I was losing my naiveté but trying to keep my sanity. And it was when I realized that I had to make it to work on time, even if I was partying the night before. And certainly it was a time when I figured out my future while finding happiness in every day.

To be honest, I'd like to say that all those things happened smoothly in my 20s. I'd like to say it, but I can't because they didn't. And that's another thing that makes your 20s today and my 20s then exactly the same. There are no smooth paths, there never have been, and there never will be. You've got to bump on down the road to get where you want, and there are some steep climbs and some gnarly switchbacks. That's the way it is, the way it always has been, and it's best that you just accept it.

# THE FOUR QUALITIES OF HAPPINESS.What is

it we are all looking for along the road to happiness? I believe it can be boiled down to four simple things: freedom; accomplishment; money; enjoyment. Put them all into forward motion, balance them and, well, my guess is they are the ingredients that will make up your happiness.

How can happiness be as simple as four qualities? Great question. As I met with my co-authors in Florida and Arizona and Massachusetts and New York and everywhere we went, the same issues kept arising. It became clear that if we took all the issues and listed them, then sorted them, they always seemed to fall into those four main categories: freedom, accomplishment, money, and enjoyment. Think about your own desires right now and you'll see what I mean. Wanting to be on your own is really about freedom, accomplishment, and enjoyment, while financial needs may be holding you back. Finding a great job is likely about enjoyment, money, and accomplishment, but you're worried about losing your freedom. Even finding the right partner is about finding someone you enjoy being with and who allows you the freedom to grow. In just about anything you want, these four qualities have to work together to allow you to be happy.

# FOUR BY FOUR

## THESE ARE THE FOUR QUALITIES
## THAT MAKE UP A BALANCED LIFE.
## LET'S LOOK AT THEM IN MORE DETAIL.

| 2006 and 1986 | We all want . . . |
|---|---|
| Freedom | We all want to live our lives free to pursue what makes us happy, what interests us, what we love. It's a big part of the American Dream. |
| Accomplishment | It feels good to know that we are contributing something to the lives of others, our family, our world, or even ourselves. We may be the only ones who know or care, or we may be recognized by others through praise, awards, and accolades. |
| Money | Whether money is a top priority or dead last on your list, we all know we have to have some to live. So whether that's a lot or a little, it's a must to be secure and get off your ramen diet. |
| Enjoyment | Everyone wants to have fun and enjoy life. That was universal in our focus groups. You have to enjoy your job, your friends and family, and the life that you choose. |

No matter what you say you want out of life, chances are it requires a combination of these four qualities. Master them all and you have balance. Allow any one of them to get too dominant and you lose your balance. So that's what this book is really about. It's about helping you survive your 20s by finding that balance between freedom, accomplishment, money, and enjoyment. Do it now and you'll understand how to keep doing it later. Blow it off now and you'll be that much further behind in the years to come. You see, finding yourself in your 20s is inevitable and it's not optional. You can't sidestep it. It happens whether or not you are ready for it and whether or not you even feel lost. The longer you put it off, the longer it will take you to find your way through it. So you may as well get started!

---

# RESOURCES

## THESE ARE SUGGESTED RESOURCES FROM BOTH 20-SOMETHINGS AND THE AUTHOR.

For a more complete list refer to Additional Resources (see page 228).

### www.NoMoreRamenOnline.com:
The place to go to hear actual excerpts from the discussions with the co-authors of this book.

# 2

# i'M SO CONFUSED

"I READ IN A MAGAZINE THAT WE LIVE IN a world of 'overwhelming choices.' No kidding. Looking for a job is overwhelming. Knowing where I want to live is overwhelming. Knowing what I want to be doing 30 years from now is really overwhelming. I don't think people can know all this in their 20s. But we are supposed to figure it out. So where do I begin?"

# THERE ARE SO MANY OPTiONS OUT THERE, i DON'T KNOW WHERE TO START. What? You

mean you're in your 20s and you still don't have the rest of your life planned out? Relax. I know very few people who do. In case you haven't already heard, I'll let you in on a little not-so-secret secret. For the rest of your life you're going to hear people saying some version of, "I still don't know what I want to be when I grow up."

I love hearing older people say it. I mean, c'mon, they're old. They already have grown up! Not so. I heard about a guy whose grandfather, a toy salesman, says with excitement that he's 86 years old and he still isn't grown up. Hearing a person say something like that tells me he still has a lot of life left in him. But to hear someone in his or her 20s say they don't know what they want to be when they grow up—well, that's pretty common. Really, it came up in every one of our discussion groups.

Thing is, I bet you have a much better idea than you think you do. Sure, when you're just starting out, there are countless options for you to pursue as your life's work—in fact, more than you even realize. But think about it, not all the options are going to appeal to you. If you're an unabashed extrovert, no way you'll be happy as a librarian. And if you can't stand to look at a checkbook, much less balance one, odds are your instincts will lead you away from anything in finance.

In our world today, choices are endless, so confusion is understandable. There's just so much information out there. That's why you have to look inside yourself first to narrow down your own world a bit. Go with your instincts and continue to narrow down the options by taking time to really get to know yourself. Take the test on the opposite page and open yourself up to your own life's possibilities.

# KNOW YOURSELF
## SELF-TEST

LET YOUR MIND GO. LET YOUR HEART TAKE OVER.
ANSWER THESE QUESTIONS AND YOU WILL FIND
CLUES TO YOUR PASSION AND THE CAREER AND
LIFE THAT WILL GIVE YOU BALANCE AND SET YOU UP
FOR HAPPINESS IN YOUR 20S AND BEYOND.

1. If money wasn't an issue for me and it was a bonus that someone would pay me, what would I spend my time doing?

2. Forget worrying about grades, these are the things people say I'm really good at. (Limit three answers.)

a. _____ b. _____ c. _____

These are the things I know I am really good at. (Limit three answers.)

a. _____ b. _____ c. _____

What were my favorite subjects and why did I enjoy them? (Limit three answers.)

a. _____ b. _____ c. _____

If I could choose anywhere in the world to live and success was guaranteed along with happiness, where would I be?

Complete this statement. "I'm happiest when I'm . . ." (Limit three answers.)

a. _____ b. _____ c. _____

For a template for the Know Yourself Self-Test,
go to the toolbox at www.NoMoreRamenOnline.com.

Pay attention to your answers because they can provide you with important clues about what makes you tick and where your passions lie. That's what it means to get to know yourself. It's a process of tuning in to those things that pique your interest and then investigating them.

When I did this self-examination years ago, even though I had graduated with math and engineering degrees, I discovered I didn't want to work behind a computer all day. I wanted to be around people more, and I wanted to be around creative people—the designers of products. With some research I found out that people like me could work for technology companies as sales and marketing engineers. That way I could be involved with the design process and around people all the time. It was a perfect fit!

Keep in mind, it's easy for me to reflect on my own experience and relay it to you in a way that sounds perfectly linear. But as you will find in your own journey, it's much more organic than that. Odds are you're not going to go away for a weekend and experience some epiphany about your life's calling, and you're not going to find the perfect job that makes it all crystal clear. Your life isn't a made-for-Hollywood script. Life is murky.

The purpose of doing some soul searching is to find a career path that matches your interests and abilities. It also will help you learn what's out there, how the world works, and how you fit in. Don't underestimate the value of devoting time to self-discovery, because the more soul searching you do now, the less likely you'll be doing it later. There's no time like the present.

# JUST WHEN i THiNK i FiGURED OUT WHAT i WANT TO DO, SOMETHiNG UNEXPECTED STOPS ME iN MY TRACKS. WiLL iT ALWAYS BE THAT WAY?

There are always obstacles, and the winners in life are the people who can overcome them, that's for sure. But the winners are also those people who can see three steps ahead and set up a game plan. Here's what I mean. If you play golf, you know that an experienced golfer doesn't just get up and hit the ball as hard as he can. Before he steps up to the tee, he analyzes the hole to figure out the best way to deal with its angles and obstacles. There's always a way to break the hole into pieces and make sure that he hits par, which is the smart plan if he is safely ahead. Then there's a riskier plan, one in which if he doesn't place the ball just right it could get him into trouble. In this case, he even thinks ahead about how he will get out of trouble if he lands there.

Your life is no different. Instead of seeing only the cup—in other words, the vision of what you want—visualize what it will take to get there to the best of your ability. Then figure out your first three moves. You may not be totally accurate, but you'll at least be more prepared. For example, if you want to become mayor, think three steps ahead. You will likely have to raise your visibility in your town. What's you're plan to get noticed? You will probably have to hold a lesser office, like town council member. What's your plan for the upcoming campaign? You will need a campaign platform. What is your vision for your town? That's looking three steps ahead and making decisions before the heat of the moment.

In the next chapter, we'll talk more about getting a plan, but for now, recognize that it is great to know what you want to

I'M SO CONFUSED

do, that's the idea! But, go one further. Begin imagining the path you will have to take to get there. Thinking three steps ahead stops you from being reactionary, it lets you lead your life instead of life leading you. And best of all, even if you're a little off in your predictions, you'll be smarter, more prepared, and happier along the way.

> My name is Mark. I am actually still in school, but at one point I was just three classes away from graduating with a degree in engineering. Now I'm not sure what I want to do, so I'm taking more classes just to figure it out. I do know one thing, though. I don't want to wake up 40 years from now and hate my life. So right now, I'm not doing much of anything until I decide. I don't know.

## I FEEL LIKE IF I JOIN THE RAT RACE IT WILL SUCK THE LIFE RIGHT OUT OF ME. I DON'T WANT TO BECOME ANOTHER WORKING STIFF.
Some career paths will immediately lead you into an exhausting schedule—one where you work more than 60 hours per week, paying your dues so you can move up the career ladder.

Unfortunately, that's the reality of many professions like doctors, lawyers, and in much of corporate America. A lot of companies say all the right things about wanting employees to maintain a work-life balance. But in the end, the boss's "What have you done for me lately?" always seems to win. That's why you see so many young, aspiring professionals on the so-called fast track scuttling around dog-tired, stressed out, and feeling like their jobs have sucked out their souls.

Now, I'm not necessarily discouraging you from working that kind of a grind. Realistically, you will have to pay some dues. Just make sure you are attentive to your surroundings and have a timeline for how long you are willing to dedicate until you transition to a more balanced lifestyle. Burnout doesn't advance anyone.

Dedicating yourself to an 80-hour, weekends-included job can be fine for a few years, provided that you're being compensated appropriately. Fact is, devoting yourself to such a schedule early in your career will likely pay long-run dividends in terms of permitting you to work at a more relaxed pace and higher pay scale later on. Just don't allow yourself to compromise your entire life for the job. In other words, sustain that anti-working stiff spirit.

I was a road warrior, traveling with my job for more than 15 years, but I didn't let my work interfere when I needed a break. I reserved time in my schedule to hang out with friends, connect with family, and exercise. When I was required to travel for work, I always carved out time—even if it was only a few hours—to see the cities I was visiting.

The working stiffs are the ones who have forgotten to do these things. They have lost focus on what they set out to accomplish (if they ever knew). Just because you choose to go to work doesn't mean you have to become a working stiff. It doesn't go hand in hand with beginning a career.

I'M SO CONFUSED

# HOW DO i FiND A JOB THAT'S FUN AND PAYS WELL?

This is one of the most common questions I hear when talking to people who are just starting out in their careers. And I am always happy to hear it, because it speaks of ambition. I mean, who wouldn't want to get paid for doing the thing they most enjoy?

When I was starting out, my original dream was to work in a job that paid me a lot of money, allowed me to see the world, and let me interface with people. Even though my degree was technical, I wanted to be in marketing or sales. I really had no passion for being a design engineer, so rather than settle, I took a marketing job with a high-tech company. And that's where I started. The pay was above average, but more than just the cash, the job gave me experience and set me on my way.

Reality check time: Most of the really fun jobs (professional sports excluded) don't pay that well—at least not when you're starting out. They aren't going to be $80,000-a-year-with-stock-options opportunities.

Odds are, you're going to have to make some trade-offs. If you decide to take a more glamorous job, say as a ski patroller, you'll certainly enjoy yourself and maintain a great social calendar, but where's that going to leave you in ten years? You may very well be struggling financially, wondering just how you let so much time pass by. It also may be more challenging and frustrating to get a career started at a later age. Younger people who were hungrier than you will be ahead.

Try to find a balance. If skiing is a passion, consider finding work off the mountain in another aspect of the ski industry (e.g., working for a manufacturer, sales, hotel management). You want to find a suitable career that you will enjoy and also provides you with sufficient money to live on, have some fun, pay off some loans, and save a few bucks, too.

The key to the fun and money equation is the idea of really knowing yourself. If you know the activities you enjoy and can find a way to weave them into your day-to-day work experience, you'll be far ahead of the pack. You may even be one of those lucky few saying, "I can't believe I get paid to do this."

If you do decide to prioritize the fun over the money, just realize it's a choice you're making and figure out a way to supplement your short- and long-term savings, because, let's face it, in the real world, we're all on our own.

# i DON'T FEEL READY TO BE MAKiNG LiFE-LONG DECiSiONS, YET. Believe me, if

you're feeling this way, you're not alone. This is such a reality for my co-authors, and I understand it perfectly. The people I've talked to see their parents or other role models having succeeded, and they just don't see how they will ever achieve comparable success having so little "real world" experience.

First, relax! You're at a major transition point in your life. Take some time to look around and breathe. If you're not ready to think in terms of the next 30 years, don't waste your time and energy fretting about it. Focus in on the next two years or the next five years, and don't sell yourself short in terms of how much you can accomplish.

So many people are afraid of so many unknowns and un- certainties that paralysis actually becomes a self-fulfilling

I'M SO CONFUSED

prophecy, and they delay taking any decisive actions. Your successful mom and dad or other role models, as you know, were once in your position, facing the same challenges that you face. Sure, times were different. For one thing, they had far fewer choices. But thoughts about starting careers and savings accounts and families—gasp!—they were just as real then as they are today.

The good thing for you is that your parents and the other people you look up to would likely jump at the opportunity to share some perspective on sticking your neck out there and making some life-guiding decisions. Why not ask them?

Meantime, remember that people make mistakes, recover, change direction, and still manage to do well. Remember your first day of college? Were you 100 percent confident that you would finish within five years? Did you know exactly what your major would be? Now here you are looking to start the next phase, and not surprisingly, you have questions.

# WHAT iF i MAKE WRONG DECiSiONS? The important thing for you to do right now is to go out there and get that first job, then navigate your way from there. No one should have to take a job that makes them miserable. But if the first step to your dream job of being a restaurant reviewer is working at the local newspaper selling ads to restaurants, then take the job. You have to start somewhere.

And once you do get started, guess what? You will make some wrong decisions. You will make some mistakes. You will take steps backward in order to step forward. The only real cause for concern is not learning from those experiences.

Take for example a guy who used to work for me. Actually, he worked for me in three different positions in four years. It took that many and a few more to realize he kept making the same mistake. He was exceptionally smart, but just couldn't get along with people. He tried marketing but couldn't get along with the sales team. He tried sales, but routinely ticked off customers. He then became a liaison between the engineers and the customers, but he felt he knew more than the engineers, so that didn't last either. My point is it took him years to discover, brilliant as he was, that he wasn't cut out to work for someone else. He was really cut out to work for himself. Finally, when he went on his own, he found himself and he found success.

If you continue to challenge yourself and try different things throughout your career and your life, from time to time you're going to make wrong decisions or try things you don't like. It goes with the territory. Don't let fear of having mud in your eye prevent you from making progress. Most people meander their way and stumble into a career, anyway. Take Jon Stewart of *The Daily Show*. He was a psychology major and got his degree in 1984 from The College of William and Mary in Virginia. His first stand-up gig was in 1987. But before that he had a bunch of different jobs, including contingency planner for the New Jersey Department of Human Services, contract administrator for City University of New York, puppeteer for children with disabilities, and bartender at the local Franklin Corner Tavern. Talk about stumbling into your life's work! That's just one example.

Having some goals will help you see the bigger picture, so you'll be better able to spot the things that might knock you off course and into wrong-decision land. I'll get to that in the next chapter.

I'M SO CONFUSED

# WHAT iF i FAiL?Warning: Hide any and all soap boxes in your vicinity, because this is where I step up with my megaphone!

Failure is part of the game. Look at Tiger Woods, the best professional golfer ever. He loses more tournaments than he wins. Look at batting averages. Even the best players hardly ever bat over .300, which means that they get out more often than they get on base.

I can appreciate your concern about failure, just the same as I appreciate people's concerns about making wrong decisions. But lead me to an entrepreneurship convention, and I'll introduce you to hundreds of people ready to risk bankruptcy despite persistent voices in their heads telling them their plans are half-baked. Show me a medical school graduation ceremony, and I'll show you row after row of people who know how to save your life—literally—but who worry they won't pass the medical board exams.

My point is that everyone, at one point or another, fears failure. But you press on anyway. Fact is, you will fail at certain times in your career—especially in the beginning. But that doesn't mean you'll wind up on the street corner washing windshields. Failure leads to learning leads to more opportunities for success. Tiger learns more from his bad shots than he does from his good ones.

Unless you continually screw up over a period of months and years, any company worth working for will continue to employ and pay you. In fact, good managers take it upon themselves to help you through the low points to make sure you learn and prosper and make good for the company.

# WHAT WORRiES YOU MOST?

## WE ASKED WHAT WORRIES YOU MOST AND THESE ARE YOUR TOP TEN ANSWERS.

1. Making a lot of life-long decisions at such an early age.

2. Self doubt—too many choices.

3. Fear of the unknown, uncertainty, and failure.

4. Finding a job I like that pays well.

5. Not finding time to enjoy life.

6. Monotony, working 9AM to 5PM.

7. Making a big mistake and not being able to recover.

8. Not making enough money to live.

9. Becoming unhappy with my job and my life.

10. Having regrets later in life.

## Now answer these questions.

### What worries you?

### What's the worst that can happen?

### How would you recover?

Part of knowing yourself is admitting your fears.
And once you know the worst that can happen,
it's not too hard to figure out what you would do.
Put a plan together, then put it away.
There's no point dwelling on the worst when
you've got it solved and in your dresser drawer.

# MY PARENTS THiNK i SHOULD PURSUE <iNSERT PROFESSiON>, BUT i REALLY DON'T WANT TO. WiLL THEY EVER FORGiVE ME?

First of all, I want to acknowledge the many cultures that are represented in the United States. My opinions, while sometimes traditional, certainly do not reflect the norm of the more patriarchal cultures. I fully recognize that even in the 21st Century, in some communities, bucking tradition and turning up your nose at the wishes of your elders just doesn't fly. Those are very real challenges for scads of people graduating into the professional world. And I'm afraid my opinions and advice may not have strong legs for people in those situations.

At the same time, I know plenty of people whose fathers or mothers have encouraged their children to pursue one career or another. Maybe they want you to join the family business. Maybe early in your college career, a professor took you under her wing and began grooming you to carry on as professor of medieval literature.

These are common scenarios and many people take comfort in having a path planned out for them. But the beauty of living in American society is freedom of choice. And maybe, just maybe, you have your own aspirations in mind.

In that case I say good for you, because I certainly couldn't have based my life's work on a direction that someone else prescribed for me—regardless of who that person was. You're the one who has to live your life. You have to follow your own passions. You have to satisfy your own ambitions first, before you can satisfy the wishes of others.

It's no different from the person who believes he or she will be happy once Mr. or Ms. Right comes along, and for that reason, continues to churn through dates, seemingly unable to be alone. People who do this either have trouble committing or are looking for happiness, purpose, and direction in someone else. But, in actuality, all of that must come from you. The same goes for your career.

My bet is your parents and the other people you look up to want you to get the most out of life—to be happy and productive—no matter how you choose to do it. No one will argue with results.

Follow your heart. Achieve success and others will have no choice but to be proud of you. Figuring out how you're going to go about achieving those results is the focus of the next chapter.

I'M SO CONFUSED

---

## RESOURCES

**THESE ARE SUGGESTED RESOURCES FROM BOTH 20-SOMETHINGS AND THE AUTHOR.**

For a more complete list refer to Additional Resources (see page 228).

http://career.sdsu.edu/MAJORS/index.htm

http://www.princetonreview.com/cte/quiz

www.careerkey.org

# 3

# i PROBABLY NEED A PLAN

"I'M A STUDENT AT ARIZONA STATE University. I completely know my definition of a dream job. It's doing something you'd do whether they paid you or not. Right now I don't know what that is for me. I love my art, but my fear is turning it into a job and having it become something I don't like to do anymore."

# RiGHT NOW MY LiFE iS LEADiNG ME.

I am a big believer in philanthropy, and one of the organizations I admire is the Leukemia & Lymphoma Society's Team in Training. The reason is two-fold. First, the program raises piles of money for an organization that works miracles. Second, Team in Training offers participants a powerful lesson on goal setting, which I believe is one of the keys to finding happiness in your 20s, and ultimately in your life.

The lesson is rooted in training for marathons and triathlons— two of the greatest tests in endurance sports. Participants begin by setting a huge goal: I will complete a marathon. Then, with all the determination and the most positive attitude they can muster, they show up for the first run. Within no time, their hearts are racing and many would-be marathoners are out of breath with agonizing side stitches. You just know the internal monologues are doing double time:

*What the heck are you doing to yourself?*
*Are you crazy?*
*Wouldn't you rather be sleeping right now?*
*Stop now before you get hurt or make a fool of yourself.*
*You can't do this!*

And in fact, many people stop right there. First run, last run. They're not committed. They listened to all the reasons why they should stop.

On the other hand, those who are serious muscle through the first run and continue pounding the pavement. Soon, one-mile morning runs become five milers. Then ten milers. Then 15. Soon enough, race day comes. They lace up, don a Team in Training jersey and eventually cross the 26.2-mile marker at the finish line, achieving the goal.

The program changes lives, not only the lives of those who benefit from the proceeds, but also for those otherwise average Joes and Janes who train and ultimately complete the races. After finishing, participants consistently remark that they have accomplished something they never believed they could do. They did it by envisioning a finish line, and working until they reached it. The lesson then spills into their personal lives, and even into this book.

## ARE CLEAR GOALS KEY? Realizing success in

your 20s—and ultimately in life—involves a similar marriage of hard work and clear goals. The journey is a marathon, not a sprint. The truth is, you can work tirelessly for years, logging 12-hour days and working when you're sick and through holidays. Without clear goals in place, however, you risk having the tasks become an endless cycle, meaningless and thankless, except to pay the bills. Don't let that happen. You have to lead your life by setting goals and going after them, rather than letting life lead you.

The good news is you already have some experience in the world of setting and achieving goals. Think about your scholastic life. The goal of graduating was built into every test you took and every paper you wrote. You did the work required of you because eventually it would bring you within reach of the goal of graduation.

Now the challenge is to identify your life goals and create a plan for achieving them. Want to be respected as a leader, some-one who makes a difference? Want to be wealthy? Want to live in Europe? Well, you have a much better shot at making these things happen if you plan for them. Goals keep you focused, so channel your ambitions by setting goals.

# HOW AM i SUPPOSED TO PLAN THE REST OF MY LiFE, WHEN i DON'T EVEN KNOW WHAT i'LL BE DOiNG FRiDAY NiGHT?

One of the most common misconceptions out there is that by the time you finish school, you're supposed to have figured out exactly what you want to do with your life. That way, you can get busy making your grand destiny happen. Talk about pressure! Not only that, but that kind of thinking is just plain wrong.

Sure, there are people in this world who have a sense from an early age about what they want to be when they grow up. They want to be pediatricians. They want to be police officers. They want to be the presidents and CEOs of Fortune 500 companies.

But for most people, it's just not that way. And if it's not that way for you, don't go beating yourself up over it. Navigating that void of not knowing the future is part of the process and the journey you're on.

In the last chapter, we talked about knowing yourself. Now we'll go a little further by starting at the end. Where do you want to end up?

Consider the marathon metaphor. You wouldn't start running without knowing where the finish line was. You'd have a clear picture of what it would look like when you got there—throngs of people cheering, finishers' medals, tables full of water and energy drinks. You'd also have a sense of what it would feel like to reach the finish line—noodle legs, utter exhaustion mixed with exhilaration, a lot of pats on the back.

Well, why should your life be any different? Why not paint a similar picture for yourself of what your life's finish line will look like? Maybe it's your professional finish line. (How will I look in a Supreme Court Justice's robe?) Or maybe it's your personal finish line. (Married with two kids, a dog, and an iguana named Spike.) Or even your finish line for giving. (That children's wing at the hospital is named after me!)

Instead of sweating over "What do I want to do with my life?," skip ahead to what your life will look like when you are successfully doing it. Then the better question to start with is, "What do I want from life?"

I was 23 years old when I first wrote down my answers to that question. I was very career focused and money was important to me, so nearly all my goals were related to career and finances. I wanted to be making more than $100,000 a year by the time I was 30. I wanted to become president of a company by age 40, and to retire, financially free, by age 45. I also wanted to make sure that I had friends to hang out with. I wanted to make sure I had time to play sports. And I wanted to see the world before I was too old to enjoy it. You might say I wanted it all. But I guess not all. I didn't really set any goals for marriage and a family; for me that came later.

I believed that working hard and making money early in my career would give me freedom later in my life. Now, I am thrilled to say that my plan paid off. I made my vision a reality. But would I have done so without having specific goals from the outset? I doubt it. I wouldn't have known where my finish line was, so there was no way I could have run toward it.

Start your own process of goal setting by painting a picture of what Success Street will look like when you get there. For me money played an important role. For you it might be giving to society, so the picture you'll paint might involve working for a nonprofit, donating your time on weekends, or being an activist for your cause. It might be fame that lights you up, in which case your picture may include getting your poetry published, having your blog get millions of hits, or having the documentary you created air on MTV or *National Geographic Explorer*.

Know what gets you psyched and aim for a comprehensive description of what would be the perfect outcome. Not only does the exercise help you identify what you want to work towards, personally and professionally, but it also helps you get to know yourself, because it highlights the things that are important to you. With this description in hand, you'll set your personal finish line and it will be easier to start figuring out how you're going to get there.

## MY GOAL iS TO BE HAPPY, EARN A GOOD LiViNG, AND EVENTUALLY START A FAMiLY. iSN'T THAT ENOUGH?

In every focus group, when I asked my co-authors to name some goals, without fail, someone would respond, "I just want to be happy." It was so universal.

The problem with such a noble goal is it's a good start, but a tad bit vague, don't you think? I mean, do you know anyone who really doesn't want to be happy?

Fact is, happiness is not a destination, it's part of the journey. It's part of the process of setting a goal that you look forward to with the same excitement you have for vacation, and enjoying the work that day by day, month by month, year by year will get you there.

# GET SOME GOALS

THE SOONER YOU GET THINKING ABOUT YOUR FUTURE,
THE SOONER YOU CAN BEGIN LEADING YOUR LIFE,
INSTEAD OF ALLOWING YOUR LIFE TO LEAD YOU.
HERE ARE SOME QUESTIONS TO HELP YOU DISCOVER
WHAT YOU WANT FROM LIFE. AS YOU WORK THROUGH
THE QUESTIONS, BE HONEST WITH YOURSELF AND
DON'T BE AFRAID TO THINK BIG!

**AGE WISH LIST:** List one or more big milestones you want to achieve by age 21, 25, 30, 40, and 50. (e.g., education, family, salary, accomplishments, giving, possessions). If you want to be a tenured anthropology professor at a major university by age 40, write it down. If you want to be a certified nutritionist, married with one child by age 30, write it down. If you want to have your first patent by age 25, write it down. Write it all down! Things may get cloudier as you try to envision your life at 50, but think of how you'd like your life to progress and aim high.

**LIFE-LONG LEARNING:** Write down the skills and experience you'll need to have under your belt to attain the milestones listed in your Age Wish List. Include ideas about how you'll get the experience (e.g., school, employer training, mentor, independent study).

**HOME BASE:** Where do you want to live (e.g., city, climate, region)? Some of your other life goals like career and school may dictate where you live, but can you identify your ultimate dream city or town?

**CAREER POSSIBILITIES:** List the careers and industries you think you might like to work in. Consider how well your education, experience, and skills would fit, as well as the future for the career and industry.

**CONTACTS:** Achieving your goals isn't just a function of what you know, it's also who you know. List the people who may be able to help you realize your dreams. Your list may include everyone from your next-door neighbor to your state senator.

**CHARITY:** Which charitable causes do you feel strongly about? Write down how you'd like to help make an impact in one year, five years, and ten years.

**SACRIFICES:** Time to be realistic and list what you are willing to postpone or give up in the short term to achieve your goals. For example, you may have to put off home ownership if you want to go to medical school.

So if the only goals you can articulate are to be happy, earn a good living, and eventually start a family, no, that's not enough. It doesn't tell you what happy looks like, feels like, or smells like. It's not specific enough to keep you motivated. It's not easily measurable. And perhaps most importantly, it doesn't provide you with a guide for making decisions.

Dig deeper. The questions included in "Get Some Goals" on the previous page can help you start thinking about what you really want. Rather than focusing on being happy, focus on the specific things that once you accomplish or acquire them will make you happy. That's what you're working towards. Decide what you want your life to be like. Write down your answers on paper. Identify the steps that will lead to your goals, and start pursuing the steps. Happiness will follow, naturally.

When your goal is an exciting destination, it's easier to stay the course, and you'll be thrilled to work toward it every day. In fact, it won't feel like work at all.

## I'D LOVE TO BECOME A SUPREME COURT JUSTICE, BUT IS THAT REALISTIC?

One of the questions I love to pose when people ask me for career advice is "What's your dream job? What would you do if you could pursue any path you wanted?"

One of my co-authors got a bit embarrassed before she said, very quietly, "I want to be a Supreme Court Justice."

I always feel sad that people are uncomfortable to admit their biggest, most ambitious dreams. It is as if saying it out loud means that if you don't achieve that, you've failed. That is not true at all. Instead, I believe you should have a larger-than-life goal—or two or three—and you should use them to motivate you to do the very best at whatever step toward it you are taking at any time. If you make it all the way, great. If you only get part way, you will know it wasn't because you didn't try your hardest.

So go on and dream big, because *the world is your oyster and you can pursue any path you want.*

Remember the story from the beginning of this chapter? The one where a guy from our focus group described a dream job as something he would be so happy doing he'd do it for free. I think that sums it up pretty well. Think about the things in your life that you love to do, that you consider play, that you would jump at the opportunity to actually get paid to do. That's how you find your dream job. I guarantee you have one, so open your mind to it.

## HOW TO FiND YOUR DREAM JOB

It's pretty simple. Just ask yourself . . .

*What do you love to do?*
*What are the ways you can be paid to do it?*

Be creative and do some research.
Too many people give up on a dream job or
dream career because they think there is no chance.

They say when you find your dream job you'll never "work" another day in your life. In reality, don't expect every day to be a holiday, but on most days you'll be happy to go to work. And many dream jobs are demanding and involve sacrifices. For instance, a lot of people think it would be great to be in the movies. However,

I PROBABLY NEED A PLAN

ask an actor and he will tell you that you have to be up early and in make up, only to stand around for much of the day while lights and cameras are adjusted and shots are reviewed. Then you have to do the scenes again and again until everyone gets them right. There's lots of pressure but also lots of waiting—and that's how it is when you do have a great movie role.

Dream jobs can be few and far between and your dream job probably won't fall in your lap. Expect to work hard at it and expect it to evolve over time. You may even need a big "break" to break the ramen cycle. However, there are steps you can take to make it happen.

## HERE'S HOW TO START ON THE PATH

- Identify all the stepping stones to your dream job.
- List all people who may be able to open some doors, or help you along the way.
- Muster up the courage to put yourself out there to open doors for yourself.
- Right now, get an insider's view of the job by getting in the door.
- Tell people what you want and that you plan to get it.

Another important reality check is if your dream job will be a good fit for you. Being a news anchor may sound good, for example, but if you aren't a morning person and you're doing a morning broadcast, your dream job might be a nightmare. Or if being a Supreme Court Justice is your dream, but you don't like politics, well, that might limit your chances of success.

Navigate the gray matter between dreaming big and fantasizing by arming yourself with the facts. Then you'll be able to determine

# ARE YOU ENTiTLED?

I'VE READ A LOT OF STORIES IN THE NEWS
ABOUT HOW PEOPLE IN THEIR 20s FEEL ENTITLED
TO THE GOOD LIFE. MAYBE IT'S PART OF COMING
OF AGE DURING THE DOT-COM CRAZE OR HAVING
PARENTS WHO WERE ABLE TO GIVE YOU A LOT.
WHETHER OR NOT IT'S TRUE—OR MORE IMPORTANTLY,
WHETHER OR NOT THE STEREOTYPE APPLIES
TO YOU—HAVING A SENSE OF ENTITLEMENT IS
A REAL DETRIMENT TO YOUR OWN SUCCESS.

**What does it really mean to be "entitled"?
You feel you are an entitled 20-something if . . .**

You feel really put out when you can't have
your Starbucks Mocha Latte every morning.

You feel like you are going way above and beyond
by working until 5:30. After five is *your* time.

You'll look for another job because
you're above "just answering the phone."

You'll blow off an interview without calling because
you decided you didn't want that job anyway.

You would never actually drive a used car.

Your monthly budget for personal maintenance rivals your rent.

You expect to have the same standard of living
that your parents have, but you're only 25.

You live at home, rent-free, and recently bought a flat-screen TV, an iPod,
a Gameboy, and a closet full of designer clothes.

You're totally okay with all of that.

if your goals and your dreams are in harmony with who you are. You'll also be able to make deliberate choices about what's going to get you to where you want to be.

One of my co-authors helped me recognize and relate an important word of caution. She said she set her goals really low so if she didn't hit them she wouldn't feel bad. A dream job was out of the question for her because a dream job involves risk. She wasn't the only one. Don't join that bandwagon. It's a great way to miss out on a lot of what life has to offer. You never know to what heights that lofty goal and your impassioned dreams can take you.

## OKAY. SO i HAVE SOME iDEAS ABOUT WHAT i WANT. HOW LONG WiLL iT TAKE?

In the go-go 90s, as you know, we experienced one of the strongest stock market run-ups in history. The Internet emerged from infancy. A raging river of initial public offerings made countless people multi-millionaires overnight. A lot of them were young— your age, now. Their careers were just beginning and already they could afford to buy flashy Porsches and gargantuan houses, fly first class, and eat dinner at Morton's.

You saw it. You know what I'm talking about. And why wouldn't you want the same thing? It's easy to see success stories like Yahoo! and expect that other opportunities for overnight riches are waiting around the corner. The hard pill to swallow about those dot-com bubble years is that they were an anomaly. If you're just starting out in your career, prepare to work hard. There will be no 18-month millionaire cash-outs from a career in which the job requirement is 20 years' experience playing video games.

Okay, you may get lucky, but that's not something you can plan on. The reality is that no matter how technology changes the way we work, we still have to work for the prize. And that takes time—years, maybe even decades, depending upon how high you set the bar for yourself.

Okay, so maybe you feel a little bit entitled. In the end, however, you will have to make it on your own. Otherwise you'll never feel a sense of accomplishment, no matter what you do or achieve. Just because you received a college degree, should you be entitled to an $80,000 salary? No, you really shouldn't, and you're not. I don't care if the degree says Harvard or Online U. On the other hand, if you condition yourself to setting goals and following through, not only will you eventually find your way to that $80,000, but it will be more satisfying because of all you did and learned to get there.

## DREAM. PLAN. EXECUTE. Remember it's a marathon, not a sprint. And just like in a marathon, one of the key stumbling blocks you will have to manage en route to your goals is the issue of commitment.

### BE HONEST WITH YOURSELF

- How long are you willing to slog it out on the front lines?
- How many hours per week are you willing to work?
- How much personal time are you willing to sacrifice?
- How willing are you to persevere?

If your answers to questions like these don't mesh with the demands of the work required to get you where you want to be, either you do have an issue with entitlement or you haven't arrived at the right goals for yourself, because you're not willing to commit to doing what it takes to get there. Sorry, those are the hard facts.

The secret to success boils down to three simple words: Dream. Plan. Execute. It's in committing to that last part—executing—where people often fall short. People are great at dreaming, have good intentions to plan, and then never actually do anything to turn dreams into reality. They dream and they hope, but that doesn't really deliver results.

You could spend hours and hours envisioning a glorious life for yourself. You could outline on paper every single step you'll need to get there and every person who can help. But if you can't commit to working the plan, regardless of how long it takes, you may as well take that piece of paper, crumple it up, and throw it in the recycle-bin.

## SHOULD i GO BACK TO SCHOOL? Statistics show
the steady increase in the number of Americans pursing advanced degrees. Their reasons for doing so are as varied as players' strategies at the World Series of Poker. For some, like doctors, lawyers, aspiring professors, scientists, and social workers, to name just a few, it's a requirement. For others it's not so cut and dried. Some are finding it difficult to get the job they want with only a college education. Others are consciously or subconsciously trying to retreat to the comfort of academia. There were even a few of my co-authors who saw school as a way to delay those inevitable school loans coming due. Still others thought of graduate school as an opportunity to hit the reset button and reinvent themselves. Don't like your job after a few years? Go back to school! Pursue a new field of study! Re-emerge as You, Version 2.0!

# BAD PLAN VS GOOD PLAN

## BAD PLAN

**Name: Jane     Location: East Lansing, Michigan**
GOAL: I want to get a better job in fashion.
CURRENT SITUATION: I'm working as an assistant manager at Banana Republic.

### MY NEXT STEPS:
1. Continue to work at Banana Republic and ask around about a better job,
maybe talk to our district manager.
2. Go to Ralph Lauren, Oscar de la Renta, etc. websites and check
for possible job openings and send my résumé.
3. Try to set up a few interviews while I'm in New York visiting my college roommate.
4. Look into taking some classes in design.
5. Get a second job at TGI Friday's to save money so I can move to New York.

### MILESTONES:
1. Complete my résumé ASAP.
2. Get trip to New York together for the spring.
3. Start scanning websites, including Monster.com, Craigslist, etc. ASAP.
4. Find a few contacts on MySpace.com who know people in fashion.
5. Save, save, save!

## GOOD PLAN

**Name: Jane    Location: East Lansing, Michigan**
GOAL: I want to be a famous fashion designer.
CURRENT SITUATION: I'm working as an assistant manager at Banana Republic.

### MY NEXT STEPS (NEXT 12 MONTHS):

1. Consider relocation to a larger city.
2. Continue my night classes in design.
3. Design my own clothes and sell to friends.
4. Get my designs carried in local boutiques.
5. Set up a website and portfolio for my designs.
6. Attend industry shows and meet at least ten new people at each.
7. Build a network of people in the industry.

### MILESTONES:
1. My own label by age 30
2. My first fashion show by age 32
3. My first magazine cover by age 35
4. My first million in annual sales by age 40

Whatever your reason, I endorse continuing your education. There's just no substitute for knowledge. I believe there's value in any educational pursuit, be it trade school, studying to be a yoga instructor, or reading up on a particular period of history. Clearly graduate school falls within the scope of this endorsement, and all things being equal, I say go for it.

But all things aren't equal. Before running out to buy a new university decal for your rear window, carefully consider a few things:

**AFFORDABILITY:** Can you manage for a while without making much money? Are you eligible for financial aid? Can you afford to accrue more debt?

**TIMING:** Would it be valuable for you to get some work experience prior to graduate school? Or is your field one where your career growth will be limited until you earn a graduate degree? Will delaying make it tougher to gain admission into your program of choice? Will work experience make it easier to get in?

**LIFESTYLE:** Are you prepared to give up free time at night and on weekends? Are you willing to sacrifice time with friends and family? Are you cool with a few more years of ramen noodles?

**MOTIVATION:** Why are you going to grad school? Is it because you really need the degree to advance your career? Because you have a burning desire? Or are you just going because you haven't found a job and you want to avoid that uncomfortable Thanksgiving banter with Aunt Lucy?

Getting more education is a great thing that you don't want to ever regret doing—or not doing. Aside from just the learning and the letters you get to put after your name, it's another opportunity to meet people in your chosen field and to grow your network. But understand your own motives, your own ability, and your own expectations of what you want out of it. You want to walk away on graduation day feeling great about the last two or more years. Take the time now to contemplate and whichever way you choose, you'll find it will be one of the best decisions you ever made.

**THiNKiNG OF GOiNG BACK TO SCHOOL? CONSiDER . . .**

*You may be paying for something your future employer will pay for.*

SOME EMPLOYERS DO PAY OR SUBSIDIZE ADVANCED EDUCATION.

*You'll owe more money when you graduate.*

MAKE SURE IT WILL BE WORTH IT.

*It may not advance you.*

JUST BECAUSE YOU HAVE A GRADUATE DEGREE DOESN'T MEAN YOU'LL ADVANCE QUICKER; THAT HAPPENS THROUGH PERFORMANCE ON THE JOB.

*It may not net you as big a pay jump as you think.*

MANY OF THE PEOPLE WE MET SAID THAT A GRADUATE DEGREE IS LIKE A BACHELOR'S DEGREE A FEW YEARS AGO; IT'S A RITE OF ENTRY.

I PROBABLY NEED A PLAN

# DO i NEED PROFESSiONAL DESiGNATiONS AND OTHER CERTiFiCATE PROGRAMS TO GET A GOOD JOB?

As you may already have discovered, in many industries, your education is simply the price of admission. The degree puts you among the pool of people who are qualified to earn the industry stripes that really matter—a Certified Public Accountant designation for accountants or a Registered Dietician designation for people in the nutrition field.

In those fields, by all means you should go out and attain the professional designations as soon as possible. Your career growth will depend on it. The same goes for real estate agents, stockbrokers, insurance agents, financial planners, and many of the technology-related positions like network administrators. Try getting a high-paying job managing Microsoft networks without being a MCSE (Microsoft Certified Systems Engineer), for example.

Meantime, there are programs out there that are less about the certificate and more about the experience you get in earning the certificate, such as the CLU designation in insurance, which stands for Chartered Life Underwriter. Those designations don't let you put Dr. in front of your name, but within their professions they signify knowledge and experience. The APR designation (Accredited in Public Relations) is another. Other accreditations are required before you can even begin working. For example, if you are going to be selling securities like stocks, you'll need your Series 7 license, and if you want to sell futures, you'll need your Series 3. There are others.

In short, get to know your industry and the accreditations and licenses you will need to advance. Sure they will cost you time and money, but if they will make you smarter, more respected, or more marketable, or get you in the game, they are well worth it.

> I thought I did everything right, I took all the right classes and even had internships during school and on breaks, lots of them. Then when I got out, I realized I needed accreditation to even be considered for entry-level jobs in my field. If I had known that a year ago, I would have taken the right steps to get my designations. Now I feel totally behind and playing catch up.

# WiLL A GRADUATE DEGREE GUARANTEE ME MORE MONEY?

This question is really impossible to answer because there are so many variables, including the field you are in and the type of position you are seeking. Then there's the question, more money compared to what? Others in your same field? Others in different fields? What would you be making without it?

But you probably want some kind of guideline, so generally speaking, most companies are apt to pay a bit more up front to people who hold advanced degrees. An obvious example of this is the starting salary for an M.B.A. versus that of someone who holds a bachelor's degree in business, finance, or a related discipline. The M.B.A. will usually be looking at more cash to start. Same goes for an M.S. in computer science or a Ph.D. in bioengineering, largely because the jobs they are seeking are more advanced. If an advanced degree helps you perform better on the job, because it makes you more knowledgeable or gives you deeper, more strategic insight, then there's a good case that a graduate degree will yield more money.

In the end there are people out there with and without graduate degrees who are succeeding and failing. There are people in higher places and lower places with and without advanced degrees. Your success in terms of enjoyment, accomplishment, money, and freedom will really come down to how you apply your education and yourself to whatever you are doing, whether it be looking for a job or working at one.

I PROBABLY NEED A PLAN

# HOW DO i PRiORiTiZE AND BALANCE MY PERSONAL OBJECTiVES WiTH MY PROFESSiONAL OBJECTiVES?

Earlier I noted that my first attempt at goal setting was extremely career focused. I was motivated by the prospect of making big money and by quickly rising to the ranks of corporate leadership. (Maybe you can identify?) Pursuing that path, of course, required some trade-offs. I missed my share of parties and had to put off marriage and starting a family. But working hard does not have to preclude time for fun.

I admit that balance has not always been my strong suit. It took missing an airplane that ultimately crashed on take off for me to get the wakeup call that life is short. Make time for all the things you love. I loved my job, so the 60- or 80-hour work weeks—the kind of effort that sometimes is required to get ahead—were okay, provided those long days were balanced with adequate doses of family, friends, rest, and relaxation. Thing is, it was up to me to reward myself with that time. After the plane incident, I got the message.

I've heard a lot of 21-year olds and even 26-year olds say they aren't ready to "give up their lives" in order to pursue a career. They'll get to their careers later, they say. Cool, if that's the choice they want to make, but let me suggest an alternative, because again, a career doesn't have to come at the expense of a life. The alternative is simple—have both. A career can actually be a great part of a life! I'm proof of that.

Why not set goals in all areas of your life—health, relationships, fun, continued education—and pursue them the same way you do your career goals? Yes, it involves a dose of reality. I mean, let's face it, work a full-time job and you won't be able to devote 50-hours a week to learning Spanish. But maybe you could take classes one or two nights a week, and participate in a conversation group on Saturdays?

Just like pursuing your dream job, balance involves commitment—no one else is keeping tabs on how often you're sneaking Oreos, or whether or not you did the sit-ups you said you would. And no one is worried about whether you're on track to make partner by 40. It's all up to you.

Balance also involves sacrifices. But if you include line items for personal objectives in your plans for each day, each week, and each month—and you attend to them—you're far more likely to find yourself going to sleep each night feeling satisfied with yourself and that you're making progress.

Bottom line is you have to enjoy working to achieve your goals just as much, if not more, than actually achieving your goals. Making time for your personal interests is part of it. And that daily enjoyment and satisfaction is one way to define happiness.

## WHAT iF i FiND MYSELF HEADiNG iN AN ENTiRELY DiFFERENT DiRECTiON FROM MY GOALS?

You've probably heard the idea of taping your goals to a bathroom mirror so you are reminded of them every day. Not a bad idea. (You may want to rethink it, though, if your goal is to make enough money to live alone and you share the bathroom with a roommate. That person may not really appreciate your tactic—either that, or it might be a great way to give a bad roommate a hint!)

Regardless of whether you keep your list of goals on the mirror or on your computer, you need to regularly set aside time to take inventory. That could be every week, every month, or every quarter, depending on how you operate. Use the time to write down all the things you have done since your last check-in that clearly lead to your goals. This is when you'll notice things like whether or not you're making progress, if you need to make adjustments, or if you're moving in a direction that's not part of the plan. You may find you have done nothing and have fallen into the realm of dreaming and hoping.

If you find you are not making the progress you had in your mind, don't get discouraged. Just take action. Perhaps you can brainstorm a different approach? Maybe the inventory was just what you needed to spring into action. If you find you are progressing faster than expected, you may want to go for bigger goals. Wouldn't that be great? Surprise yourself!

Having goals helps you recognize when you're veering off track. You'll be able to determine whether or not the direction shift is a good thing or a not so good thing. After all, there are many roads that lead to your future. Maybe great opportunities that you couldn't have foreseen presented themselves and you seized them. That took you off track. Maybe your priorities are changing, in which case get used to it—all through your life, your priorities will change! I know people who were completely career driven, then met the right person, got married, had kids, and, guess what? Family came first, career took a backseat. Nothing wrong with that.

Of course, maybe the different direction is not so positive, which also is part of the game. I know one guy who gave up a job with a great future to partner with a friend on a long-shot start-up. He invested everything and when it crashed and burned, he had to start over. Setbacks happen. Don't waste too much time or energy dwelling on the fact that you failed or the failure itself. Take time instead to figure out what went wrong, learn from it, and then figure out a game plan to get you back on track. Failure by many people's standards, mine included, is a good thing. You'll come out of it wiser and stronger.

As I said earlier in this chapter, one of the real powers of having goals is they keep you focused. They also keep you motivated. I'm not sure where I would be without goals, and that's the point. Goals get you where you want to go and help you create a path. When you attach time limits to them and do what it takes to achieve them, you'll be shocked by what you'll accomplish personally and professionally. I guarantee.

## RESOURCES

### THESE ARE SUGGESTED RESOURCES FROM BOTH 20-SOMETHINGS AND THE AUTHOR.

For a more complete list refer to Additional Resources (see page 228).

www.thegoalguys.com
www.mygoals.com
www.mindtools.com
www.teamintraining.org

I PROBABLY NEED A PLAN

# 4

## i WANT
## THE RiGHT JOB

"WHEN I GRADUATED I GOT A JOB WITH a large bank in the telemarketing department. At first it was okay, but then it got really boring and I began to hate it. I decided to quit and look for another job, but that hasn't been very easy. Now I'm helping out on some construction jobs and have been for about a year. I decided to join the Navy. I think I want to be an intelligence officer. I leave for basic training in two weeks. I'm pretty excited about it."

# TRUST iN YOUR POTENTiALWhen I graduated

college and began my journey in business, Ronald Reagan was president of the United States, most telephones had cords, and one of the things consuming my friends' and my attention was a new (and wildly addictive) video game called Pac-Man. I know, it actually was the last century.

Well, back in the 20th Century when I was starting out, career advice was as generic as Wonder Bread: Write a one-page résumé. Find a good company. Work hard for 25 years. Take your gold Rolex and retire to the sidelines. But this mirror of the model life was beginning to see signs of cracking. Things like mergers and acquisitions triggered white collar layoffs and the 80s ended on the brink of tough economic times.

Don't worry, I'm not about to push the "play" button on my cassette player and start rocking to Flock of Seagulls while downing a Bartles and Jaymes. I'm just reminiscing to show how different the landscape was for me, compared to what you're facing, and at the same time, so much the same.

Yet, when it comes down to starting a job search, most of the things on the minds of my co-authors are not so drastically different from the things that were on my own. There are worries about finding a job that's exciting and about convincing employers that you're the right candidate for that exciting job. Then there are worries about being able to do what it takes to keep that job. There are worries about how long the job search may take and whether or not you will have to clean houses, bartend, or do some other part-time job to make ends meet. How long will the temporary life go on?

Maybe you face the prospect of having to move to a new city. Maybe you fear having to adopt a corporate drone mentality just to fit in. Anyone can do that for a while but you probably don't want to actually become a corporate drone.

I had similar worries when I was first starting out, and my friends had similar worries. Depending on the hour or who we were talking to, we could be excited, insecure, or flat out overwhelmed. What I never doubted, though, was my potential. And here's an important point: It's your potential that really matters in the beginning.

Even though you may think you learned a lot in college, companies that recruit you and your comrades aren't necessarily interested in what you know right now. They're interested in what you can learn and what you can—sooner rather than later—contribute. They are interested in your potential. Keep this in mind as you draft your résumé and prepare for job interviews.

## i HEAR MONSTER.COM JOB LiSTiNGS GET THOUSANDS OF RESPONSES. HOW DO i LAND MiNE AT THE TOP?

No doubt the most radical change in the job-hunting landscape in the 21st Century has been the evolution of Monster.com and other online job resources. It doesn't take a genius to know that websites have caused want ad sales to take a hit. In fact one report says that job ads on Monster, HotJobs.com, and CareerBuilder.com outstripped their newspaper counterparts three to one. And why should we be surprised? Today you don't need to wait for listings in the Sunday paper. You can search for jobs anywhere in the world and respond to listings 24 hours a day, 7 days a week, and 365 days a year.

If you ask me, I say it's both a blessing and a curse. The upside, obviously, is you can find out about new opportunities every

I WANT THE RIGHT JOB

day, without even leaving your email inbox. You can program the sites to send you alerts as soon as new postings come in that fit what you're looking for. That's the power of technology.

The problem, however, is that these sites seem to imply that finding a job is a cinch. At any given time, Monster alone has hundreds of thousands of jobs waiting in its database. A person with your skills and your education and your personality should have no problem landing one, right? Well, kudos to those who experience it that way, but for most, as you may know, it's just not that easy. The fact is most people find jobs through a network or referral.

## MONSTER.COM CONFiRMS NETWORKiNG ROCKS

An online poll by Monster.com revealed 46 percent of the 22,272 respondents found jobs through peers and friends. And 91 percent of 10,000 voters found networking to be an important component to any job search.

The Society for Human Resources Management's study got similar results. They said 90 percent of jobseekers used networking in conjunction with their job searches.

That's why I find putting your hopes and dreams into a website alone is a bit risky at best and demoralizing at worst. Get out and meet people rather than stay glued to the online job listings or your email inbox every second of the day just so you can be one of the first to find and respond to a hot lead. Scanning these listings all day is overwhelming, and it's unhealthy and unproductive.

If nothing else, I suggest that you don't fixate on being first in the queue and here's why: First of all, you have to consider what's happening on the other side of the listing—the hiring side. If it's a small or medium-size company you're responding to, I guarantee there's no one sitting at a desk on the other side, patiently waiting for responses to the ad. The person who posted the listing probably is swamped covering both his or her own job and the one you're applying for. He or she probably checks for responses once or twice a day and stacks them (digitally or in printouts) so he or she can pick through them all at once. No one is responding to résumés as they come in, or at least very few are.

If it's a large corporation, odds are you're responding to a computer that's been programmed to search your résumé for relevant key words. The computer doesn't discriminate between who came in first versus who came in 201st. All it worries about is which one has the most key words.

All this to say, getting your response in first, by itself, is not likely to make a difference. So don't worry about it. Step away from your computer. Keep a healthy balance in your schedule. Respond within a few days of the listing and you'll be fine.

The fact that computer bots play a part in the résumé screening process should further influence you to not bend over backwards trying to figure out how to ace the online job sites. How frustrating to think that you could spend hours crafting a beautiful cover letter, making sure it oozes with personality and is a model of grammar and punctuation, only to have a computer trash the letter within a split second because it doesn't have all the right key words. If you're responding to job postings online, your cover letter or résumé better echo key elements of the job description.

## ONE RÉSUMÉ OR MULTiPLE RÉSUMÉS?

### THE QUESTION

Should I have one résumé that fits all or multiple
résumés tailored to the different jobs I apply for?

### THE ANSWER

Today, it's easy to have multiple résumés,
each targeted to the qualifications for each job.

### BUT A BIT OF ADVICE

If one résumé doesn't fit all needs, and you feel you need multiple
versions, keep track of which version you send where.
Mess that up and it could cost you a job.

Another important thing for you to recognize is that job sites
are more interested in getting the listings than in getting you
a job. You are on your own, so I encourage you to temper your
expectations of these sites and curb any fixation on trying to
master them. If you approach these sites thinking you're going
to get tons of job interviews, you may be very disappointed.

But go ahead, scan the jobs. Submit a few résumés. You may
get lucky. To me though, the real value of these sites is in the
insight you glean from the language of the listings themselves,
from the other resources the sites provide, and from an aware-
ness of the shear number of job options. How do you know
that you want to be a logistics planning specialist if you didn't
know the job existed? Monster keyword searches can open up
a world of potential jobs you probably never heard of, but that
just might lead you in the right direction.

Not only do Monster and its brethren offer pages upon pages of jobs and job descriptions to broaden your horizons about what's out there and what you might like to pursue, they offer so much more. Listings on the sites convey the language that people in your desired field use to describe the industry, their company, and the work they do. Forums let you trade tips with other jobseekers, how-to guides give you job search basics, and résumé help does just that.

Take advantage of this information. Read discussions about the companies you're interested in. Borrow the language that appears on the site as you craft your own résumé and cover letter and as you talk to people who may know people who may know of a job opportunity that's perfect for you. Use these sites for what they most have to offer: information and knowledge to make you a smart jobseeker.

## I'VE HEARD ABOUT THE "HiDDEN" JOB MARKET. WHAT EXACTLY DOES THAT MEAN? HOW DO i TAP iT?

I've already sounded off on why I believe Monster and the other online job sites are valuable but likely not your best bet for finding the job that's right for you. My opinion is that people really help other people get jobs. That's right, your friends, family, professors, and colleagues are your best bet.

They also may know people with whom you should talk about your particular field of interest. Maybe one of those people knows of an opening. Or maybe he or she knows someone else you should talk to and that person knows of an opening. These are the jobs that aren't listed on career sites, the so-called hidden job market. It's the way people get jobs and it's happening daily among people you know. Later you'll see how you make contact, but for now, commit yourself to making an effort to meet people and learn who and what they know.

> **I met a finance student.**
> Her dream job wasn't to become a high-powered banker on Wall Street, although those firms would have been lucky to have her. Instead, she wanted to go into microfinance, a field relatively unknown to most. There are few jobs posted for positions in microfinance, so how did she manage to set herself up with multiple job opportunities? By working the hidden job market. Through her professors, the colleagues they knew and other business professionals, she got her start.

As that story suggests, you can reap numerous benefits by devoting your career search efforts to the hidden job market. Here's how you do it:

It starts with knowing what you want and being able to communicate it. One of the reasons I addressed goal setting (see Chapter Three) prior to this chapter is because you really have to be able to articulate your interests and your desires before someone else can help you fulfill them. It's the difference between a person saying, "I want to find a job," and another person saying, "My dream is to work for an aerospace company designing rocket engines." Who's easier to help? I have friends who can help the budding rocket scientist. It's a lot tougher to start helping the other person.

You have to know your dreams and be able to tell others what you want, what you like, dislike, and what you aspire to. If you can articulate this to someone, chances are they or someone

NO MORE RAMEN

8

they know can help you get there. I can't over-emphasize the importance and power of the goal-setting process.

Next, you put the ball in motion. Tell friends, family members, professors, and colleagues about your goals. Ask if they know someone you could talk to. Ask if they'd be willing to pass along that person's contact information, or even make the introduction. And then ask the contact if they can spare even 30 minutes for an informational interview. Through informational meetings you get perspective on how your skills may fit, including skills you may never have thought would be applicable. You'll probably learn about jobs that you never knew existed.

## STEP-BY-STEP iNFORMATiONAL iNTERViEW

### HERE'S THE FACE-TO-FACE PROCESS:

Schedule the meeting.

Treat it like an interview.

Share copies of your résumé and, if appropriate, work samples.

Ask thoughtful questions (prepare them in advance).

Respect the clock, so you're not consuming more of the person's time than you said you would.

Ask if they know someone else it might make sense for you to talk to.

Follow up with a thank you (via email or hand-written note).

Contact the referral.

Repeat.

Notice how different, and in some ways how similar, networking in person is when compared with the networking you probably already do online. It's still all about building a relationship and communicating. Except that in person you get that face-to-face contact. You get to drive or walk up to a building and get a feel for the kind of business and even the kind of person. Is the building modern? Is it clean? Is it in a good part of town? These are all clues of legitimacy. On the other hand, through sites like MySpace.com and even Monster's networking areas, you have to be more on your guard. Is that person who says he is an associate producer with MTV really a producer with MTV? I know one person who carried on a two-month-long conversation with a guy who said he was a producer for ABC News only to find he was a wacko who had nothing to do with ABC or any other media acronym. They're out there.

## STEP-BY-STEP iNFORMATiONAL iNTERViEW

### QUESTIONS TO ASK DURING AN INFORMATIONAL INTERVIEW

Whether you're meeting face to face or talking online, these are questions worth an answer:

What's it like to work in your field?

How did you get started?

What advice would you have for someone starting out today?

What skills or experience will I need for the job?

Is there anyone you suggest I contact to find a job?

Pursuing work this way, especially in person, is less intimidating than in an official interview, and it's a great way to practice your interviewing skills without all the pressure. When you meet with a friend of a friend, there's less ice to break—the conversations inevitably start with compliments or funny stories about the common friend. This makes things more personal, even casual, and from there you're off and running.

Working the hidden job market also is more gratifying for you and the people you meet. For you, it's a way to start building a network and receive affirmation about the career you're interested in. It's a way to learn the ropes from people who are balancing careers and personal lives. Plus, the feel-good value can't be beat: The people you reach out to will actually return your phone calls!

For the people you meet with, trust me, they will love the opportunity to play expert. People relish giving advice, particularly to someone who is genuinely interested in hearing it and taking it. Sometimes if they end up hiring you, they can make a few bucks. Have you ever heard of referral bonuses? Some companies have them. But seldom is it about the money. As you advance in your career, you'll also learn there are few things as gratifying as helping someone to get on their way. The more energy you invest in tapping the hidden job market, the more likely it will yield the kind of things you're looking for.

## WHAT SHOULD i LOOK FOR iN AN EMPLOYER?

When you were in school and just looking for a paycheck, the best job likely was the one that put the most money in your pocket. Starting out in a career, though, looking for that first "real" job, it is not so straightforward. Yes, you want to be paid well. But you also have to consider that this is a place where you'll spend most of your waking hours. Among other things, you want to know that your employer cares about people and has a purpose, but that's just one important aspect.

Here I've listed some key areas to research, some ideas about what the research will tell you, and where you can begin your search.

**INDUSTRY:** Is the industry growing, flat, or declining. If you get your choice, choose a growth industry; why work in an industry that is prone to massive layoffs? Some industries are consolidating, which means companies are buying each other. Still others are sending jobs overseas. This could mean instability, too. One person I met spent ten years in telecommunications only to find herself backtracking in her career because companies in that industry are merging and cutting back. Recognize first that all industries are not equal, then evaluate where the company you're considering falls.

**MARKET:** The market is the place where a company sells its products. Is it one you'll enjoy? Is it growing or declining? Are there lots of companies selling to this same group of customers? If you're a sports nut, why work for a company that markets infant car seats? Find a company that markets its products to sports enthusiasts, people like you. It'll be a lot more fun. Again, look for markets that are growing and where competition is healthy. That signals opportunity. Watch out for markets that are overcrowded, which could make growth difficult and could foretell industry consolidation.

**DIVERSIFICATION:** List the products or services and the markets each serve. If there are lots of different markets and lots of different products, the company is diversified. Diversified companies pose less job risk, generally speaking, and more opportunity to move from one division to another, if necessary. Examples of diverse companies are General Electric, with their many divisions, but also Starbucks with its many products and sales outlets. If the company you're considering is not diverse, do they have plans to venture into other areas?

**REVENUES:** It's always better to work for a company that is making money than one that isn't. Let's face it, getting paid is kind of important. Does the company you're considering have a track record over the past few years of bringing in more money than its competitors? What are they projecting for the future? Is it a reasonable projection? Some companies, Amazon.com, for example, ran in the red for years and still made payroll—but that isn't the norm.

**PROFIT:** Bringing in revenue is one thing, but profits are another. Is the company spending money faster than it is bringing it in? If so, the company is not profitable and will likely have trouble growing. If after expenses and taxes, there is money left over, that's profit and more is better when it comes to job stability. What are their profitable products, and how long can the gravy train last? How do their profits compare with the competition's? When given the choice, look for companies that turn a profit or a non-profit that has good financials.

**PRIVATE OR PUBLIC:** I really believe that early in your career, big public companies may still be a safer bet since they tend to be more stable, regimented, and have better benefits than smaller private companies. They tend to be great training grounds, but sometimes may only give you narrow experience in contrast to smaller companies, where you may be creating a plan for a new product one minute and taking out the garbage another. But keep in mind, there are some very successful private companies, such as M&M/Mars, and also struggling public companies like General Motors. Bigger doesn't always mean better.

**THE BUZZ**: What are people saying about the company? Will you be proud to say where you work or who you work for? Look for articles about the company by doing an on-line search. Ask around. Avoid companies with negative press, unless you like a challenge. The book *Anatomy of Greed* about the Enron scandal, is an extreme example of this point. Once the bad news about the company surfaced, their business and the careers of many innocent people came to a screeching halt. Later in your career you'll find that big payoffs can come your way if you can turn around a company on a downward skid. But you never want to be associated with companies that are unethical.

**CULTURE**: What's it feel like to work in this company? How do things get done? How flexible are the work hours? What kind of leader is the person in charge? What's expected of you while on the job? All this and much more adds up to what's known as "culture." It's probably the hardest aspect to actually get a handle on until you walk in the company and talk with people, but it's also one of the most important. You'll want to find a company with a culture that's comfortable for you. The best you can do is ask about the company's core values and then follow your gut once you walk through the door.

**IMAGE**: How does the company look, from its building to its promotional materials? Are people's workspaces neat or trashed? Is their online image professional? Is the company a good community citizen? It all matters because your name will be attached to this place for years via your résumé with whatever image the company has—good or bad.

Consider all these things and compromise a bit because, realistically, you'll have to. But one thing's for sure, never compromise on ethics.

# WHAT'S MOST IMPORTANT IN A BOSS

One of the aspects my co-authors found most important, aside from doing something they loved, was working with a good manager. Right Management Consultants asked workers what qualities are most valued in bosses.

## HERE'S WHAT THEY FOUND OUT

| | |
|---|---|
| Good Communication Skills | 47 percent |
| Sense of Vision | 44 percent |
| Honesty | 32 percent |
| Decisiveness | 31 percent |
| Good relationships with employees | 26 percent |
| Intelligence | 23 percent |

# WHAT SHOULD i LOOK FOR iN A JOB? Already

I've alluded to one of the concerns that seems to come up time after time for people just starting out—the fear of becoming another working stiff, trudging through the week with little more than a heavy step and a just-kill-me-now expression.

The working stiffs of the world are the people who have lost passion in their day-to-day occupation. Maybe their jobs are too easy or painfully monotonous and they are just doing it for the money. But really, a lot of it has to do with the individual not making the most of his or her time.

Certainly part of becoming complacent in your job is not being hungry enough to actively seek to fill your plate with activities and tasks that you find interesting and that keep you motivated. Ideally, these are the qualities you want to look for in a job.

Money pays the bills, but true happiness in your work goes well beyond the dollars. In fact very few of the co-authors for this book felt money was the most important part of their jobs.

In addition to working for and with good people, you want to find a position where you'll be able to start building a track record of results, successes, and accomplishments. This is because at your first job—and every job thereafter—you're not only working to learn everything you can, but also to build bullet points on your résumé. Bullet points equal accomplishments and accomplishments lead to more confidence and a more sought-after you. Bullet points set you up for the future.

Keep in mind, though, that building a great set of credentials doesn't happen overnight. Look for a job that you can envision yourself doing for a couple years. Job stability early in your career is a definite plus.

Now, having spelled out the ideal, I also have to acknowledge the Nike factor—just do it. When it comes to entering the world of "real jobs," you have to just do it. Odds are, you'll face the rude awakening that most entry-level positions are not glamorous. You won't have a seat at the important meetings. When bonus day comes, your check won't have more than three zeros— maybe not even more than two. But a start is a start.

Just do it. Look for a job that's going to give you the best chance to build bullet points on your résumé and set you on your path.

## SOME IDEAS ABOUT WHAT THAT JOB MIGHT LOOK LIKE

- Job is at a company that's growing and that promises opportunities for advancement.

- Job is at a company that has a strong reputation in the industry and solid management, including your direct boss.

- Job involves a product or service that you are interested in.

- Job involves working with others who seem happy, positive, motivated, and are generally nice to work with.

- Job-related commitments, such as hours, deadlines, travel, are acceptable.

Again, you'll have to make compromises. It's important to know what you're willing to sacrifice to achieve your goal. Then, it's time to just go for it . . . or should I say, just do it!

# iF THE PERSON HiRiNG iS ONLY GOiNG TO LOOK AT MY RéSUMé FOR A SPLiT SECOND, HOW iMPORTANT iS iT, REALLY?

Imagine yourself home on a Friday evening. It's been a long day. You're tired and hungry. As you start to munch on a few pretzels, you realize you don't know what you really want to eat. You mentally run through your list of regular haunts. Burgers, nah. Pizza, no. Nothing. Then you dive into a stack of menus and coupons you have stashed in a drawer, discarding one after the other. Too fattening, too boring, not good. Then something clicks: *Ah yes! Chinese chicken salad. That's it!*

The menus and coupons were your weed-out tools to determine what you wanted to eat.

Well, when it comes to finding employees that's what your résumé is, too. It's a weed-out tool. Just as you looked at the menus, people look at your résumé—yes, briefly at first—for reasons why you're *not* a good candidate. Not enough experience. Too many different jobs. Can't spell. That's why it has been hammered into your head, time after time, to pay attention to detail and not have any typos or other blatant imperfections on your résumé.

Sure all your information is on the page, but what's your résumé say when read between the lines? Organized? Responsible? Detail oriented? Focused? Bright? Well rounded? The idea of a résumé is not to reveal every detail about yourself, but to briefly tell the reader: (1) what you've accomplished, (2) why that makes you unique, and (3) how that can translate into a benefit for your supervisor and any company smart enough to hire you.

Few employers will hire based on the résumé alone, but they're more than willing to weed out candidates that way. Your résumé is important because often it's your only way of getting into the "let's interview" pile.

Remember, at this point, it's all about your potential. The entire résumé process—and the subsequent interview process—is an exercise in showcasing how much you can learn later.

So ask yourself, what's the picture you're painting in your readers' minds? Years back, I got a résumé from a guy who was interested in a job I had available. His résumé looked great. It was nicely formatted. There were no misspelled words. He used action words to communicate his accomplishments, and he had interesting experiences.

The problem was how he described two of the experiences.

- **Barker on a Jersey Shore pier**
- **Bartender at a topless club**

Now, as you know, when you're in college and you need money, a job is a job—you go for the cash. That's fine. The problem here was that he paraded these two job experiences as ugly ducklings. If you can't figure out a way to put a positive light on a job, leave it off the résumé. He could have simply said he was a sales promoter for a store on the Jersey Shore pier, and that he tended bar to earn college money. His choice to share the overly colorful details of the jobs showed an error in judgment and, for that reason alone, I weeded him out. He obviously didn't understand a business audience or that these two job experiences sounded seedy. There was no way that I would risk him making a judgment error with our clients. He made one; he could make another. I read between the lines and tossed him in the "do not interview" pile.

Now, keep in mind the fine line between painting a nice picture and overselling yourself. Regard the latter as a real taboo; even white lies about your experiences inevitably will haunt you.

There's no point in suggesting that at age 24 you're running an entire company, if that's not the case. Everyone knows 24-year-old entrepreneurs are few and far between (and not looking for jobs). Keep it real. Focus the attention on how you are contributing, what makes you desirable, and what your résumé says about you.

When I put together my very first résumé, I didn't think I had much relevant experience. But instead of trying to wordsmith my tasks to make them sound super important, I decided the best thing to do was call a duck a duck. That meant rather than trying to be someone I wasn't, I'd show to the best of my ability who I was.

Here are two surprising things I put down with great results:

## WHAT I INCLUDED

- Worked my summers as a construction worker during college.

- Helped my family with their coffee distribution business.

## WHY THEY LIKED IT

- Showed a willingness to work hard, and that I wasn't above performing manual labor. Also made for good conversation when they found out I operated a jack-hammer.

- Demonstrated a good family foundation and a willingness to help people and work weekends and long hours. Provided a platform to discuss how I grew to handle inventory, cash flow, and a weekly route of customers. Showed solid responsibility at a young age.

# RÉSUMÉ SUCCESS

A GOOD FIRST CONTACT CAN GIVE YOU A CHANCE
AND A BAD ONE CAN TAKE YOU OUT OF THE RUNNING
ENTIRELY. HERE'S HOW TO AVOID THE PROFESSIONAL
WORLD'S VERSION OF "DO YOU COME HERE OFTEN?"

Email your résumé and cover letter.

Contact interviewer directly to follow up.

Use professional phone manner.

Be brief.

Land the interview, hang up, celebrate (in that order).

Begin interview preparations.

# INTERVIEW PREP

ONCE YOU LAND THE INTERVIEW, HERE'S HOW
TO MAKE SURE YOU GIVE IT YOUR BEST EFFORT.

Google typical interview questions and prepare answers.

Research the company.

Have your own questions prepared.

Select your outfit.

Do a dry-run drive-by if needed, so you don't get lost.

Look your best.

Arrive early.

Be positive, flexible, and willing.

Here are some other ways to take typical jobs and give them some shine:

**WAITRESS AT OLIVE GARDEN:** Delivered the ultimate service experience and made sure that every customer I served was 100 percent satisfied.

**SALES CLERK AT X-TEAM:** Became expert in all skateboard, accessory, and apparel product lines. Determined each customer's needs and matched those needs to the best products for them.

**SKI INSTRUCTOR:** Attained my Certification Level 1 designation and taught new adult skiers basic and advanced skills through great communication, demonstration, positive reinforcement, and fun.

**HOUSEKEEPER:** Exceeded the expectations of four families by going above and beyond to make sure their homes were clean, fresh, and welcoming when they returned. Built relationships with all families and enjoyed a high level of trust.

As you can see, it doesn't take over-the-top experiences and descriptions to make a résumé interesting or to demonstrate potential. It does, however, take great work on the job. The last thing you want is to spin your job with a bunch of lies. These jobs and their descriptions are loaded with the kind of potential employers are looking for including: passion, commitment, willingness to learn, caring, follow-through, communication, service, etc. It's all about potential, and your résumé often is an employer's first clue.

# WHAT CAN i DO TO iMPRESS THE PERSON WHO iNTERViEWS ME?
The first thing is the first impression. Make a good first impression and by that I mean in the first minute or less, and you'll have a chance at the job. So

# iNTERViEW PREP FORM

## USE THIS KIND OF FORM TO HELP YOU GET ALL THE INFO YOU NEED BEFORE THE INTERVIEW.

### THE COMPANY

Reputation_____

Public vs. Private_____

Sales History (3 Year)_____

Profit History_____

### PEOPLE

Executive Backgrounds_____

Supervisor Background_____

Friends/Family at Company_____

### PRODUCTS

Products or Services_____

New Product_____

Competitors_____

### CUSTOMERS

Current Customers_____

Target Customers_____

Customers' Perceptions_____

To downlaod a template for this form,
go to the toolbox at www.NoMoreRamenOnline.com

# WHAT NOT TO WEAR

INTERVIEWERS LOOK FOR INSTANT SIGNS
THAT WILL SIGNAL YOUR ATTENTION TO DETAIL,
AND YOUR LEVEL OF CARING AND COMMON SENSE.
WHERE DO THEY FIND THEM? OFTEN IN YOUR APPEARANCE.

## GROOMING

Do you look clean, fresh, and pulled together?
If you've got a funky haircut or color, it's best to calm it down for the interview.

## STYLE

Is the cut of suit, shirt, blouse, skirt professional and suited to your body type?
Is the suit of this era? If not, invest in a new one. Don't show too much of
your body at any point—arms, cleavage, midriff, upper leg.

## FABRICS

No spots, wrinkles, or clashing patterns.

## ACCESSORIES

Nothing overwhelming or dominant. Leave your big bag at home;
carry a classic bag, briefcase, or portfolio instead. Make sure all
your leather accessories match or work together.

## METAL AND JEWELRY

Do your metals match or at least work together? Is your bling blinding?

## SHOES

For men, are the shoes professional, polished, and not overly worn.
For women, find the balance between frumpy and sleazy,
but err toward frumpy if you have to.

## PIERCINGS AND TATTOOS

If you've got them, take them out or keep them covered.
Some managers won't care, but many will, and you have no way
of knowing until you meet, which, of course, is too late.

Note that these are recommendations that will improve your chances of finding a job.
There are some careers where a little eclecticism is a plus. Or you may be a person
who says, "They either like me for me or they don't, even with my Mohawk."
Just don't be upset if they like you, but the Mohawk is a deal breaker.

let's start right off with appearances. I know that may seem superficial, but it's reality.

I'll never forget one person I interviewed years back—and I remember him for all the wrong reasons! During our first interview, he said everything right. He had the qualifications I was looking for. It seemed a great fit—except for his suit. It was behind the times; wrinkled, let's just say it was a bit out of character for the position.

Well, not wanting to make a snap judgment, I invited him to lunch a few days later. And to my shock—and horror—he showed up wearing the exact same suit. No lie! At least it made my decision easy.

It's not that I think crimes of fashion imply that people are bad or that they are potentially low performers. Rather his bad suit made a bad first impression, which I tried to overlook. But then his choice to wear the same suit for the second meeting told me he lacked basic judgment. It told me he didn't care about appearances, which made me question how he would present himself to customers and what the quality of his work would be. It also showed a lack of resourcefulness. I mean, c'mon! Borrow a suit for heaven sake! Borrow a couple hundred bucks. Do what it takes to make a good impression!

Needless to say, he didn't get the job.

In this world, appearances count—a lot! We've all sized up people based on their appearances. And sometimes, after having the luxury of time to get to know a person, we also learn our first impressions were way off. But when it comes to interviewing, unless you nail it the first time, there is no luxury of the getting-to-know-you phase.

It's been said that an interviewer will sum up whether you're a viable candidate for a job in the first minute of an interview. That's nothing but appearances and the first few words out of your mouth.

## CONSIDER THESE GUIDELINES

- Strive for an above-average appearance.

- Polish your greeting and your handshake.

- Arrive early and wait in the lobby if needed (you'll appear calmer).

- Assemble a first interview outfit and a second interview outfit.

- Err on the conservative side.

- Get business cards from everyone you meet.

Of course, appearances are just part of the package. Let's assume you pass the first impression test. To win over an interviewer, you'll also need to supplement your polished appearance with confident words.

## INTERVIEW BASICS

- Don't exaggerate. It just gets you in trouble.

- Lose "totally" and "so" and "like" and all other casual adjectives from your dialogue, as in "I'm like, so totally not going to screw up this interview." Use them and you will screw up the interview. I mean, duh! (Avoid that one too.)

- Communicate your accomplishments clearly and concisely.

- Take credit for your work humbly; sell without bragging.

- If the interviewer wants to talk GPA, talk GPA, just make sure it's real.

- Ask questions too; this is your chance to get to know the company and your potential supervisor.

- Get the interviewer to talk about a subject of interest to him or her. It helps forge a relationship.

# RATE THE EMPLOYER

**YOU MAY NEED TO DECIDE BETWEEN MORE THAN ONE JOB OFFER, SO MAKE SURE YOU TAKE A FEW MINUTES RIGHT AFTER THE INTERVIEW TO WRITE DOWN YOUR IMPRESSIONS. HERE ARE A FEW THINGS TO CONSIDER.**

## THE JOB

Job Description _____

Interesting Tasks, Duties _____

Working Hours _____

Travel Requirements _____

## THE PEOPLE

Impression of Interviewer _____

Impression of Co-Workers _____

## THE ENVIRONMENT

Offices and Workspaces _____

Equipment and Organization _____

Overall Feeling _____

Corporate Culture _____

## THE PAY AND BENEFITS

Pay (Salary, Bonus, Commission) _____

Benefits (Self, Family) _____

Retirement—401K (Matching) _____

Stock Purchase Plan _____

Relocation (If Required) _____

Vacation _____

Advancement Prospects _____

My Interest Level 1–10 (10 being the best) _____

Why? _____

To downlaod a template for this form,
go to the toolbox at www.NoMoreRamenOnline.com

Much of interview success is common sense and knowing what to expect. It requires diligent preparation and a good measure of selling yourself. Again, you're selling potential. The interviewer's ultimate goal is to make an educated guess about how quickly you will develop, how well you'll get along with others, and how soon and how much you will contribute to the company.

Use the interview time to erase any shreds of doubt about your ability to do those things, and you'll be well on your way to getting your foot in the door.

## SHOULD i EMAiL MY THANK YOU NOTE OR WRiTE iT ON PAPER?

First off, yes, thank you notes are essential. I am amazed at how many people overlook this aspect of the interview process. The notes don't have to be long—in fact, they shouldn't be. But it is a courtesy that you can use to further tip the scales in your favor. Thank you notes say volumes about your attention to detail and respect for others' positions and time.

Sending via email versus paper is basically a judgment call, but realize the immediate nature of email may give it the advantage over other methods. Be sure to include a professional email signature with your full name, address, and phone.

If it's a technology job, or one that makes heavy use of technology, email probably is the more appropriate route. If you do send a thank you via email, make sure your email address doesn't send the wrong impression. Partyanimal242@partypants.com, for example, probably would do more harm than good. If nothing else, use a free email service to establish a more professional-sounding address.

Sending a thank you by mail can convey a more refined message even if it takes longer to get there, and it can be done in addition to or in place of email. Just be sure you choose stationery that makes the right statement. Monogrammed stationary is a perfect call.

If you send the thank you by email, do it immediately so it arrives the same day or at the latest the next day. If you are sending the thank you by mail, make sure it reaches the intended recipient within three days. Your best bet is to write it as soon as possible after the actual interview is over. If you wait even a day, you risk letting it slip to the back burner and then you may forget. Not only that, but you may forget what you wanted to reinforce from your interview.

## HOW TO WRITE A THANK YOU NOTE

HERE'S A TYPICAL FORMAT FOR THANK YOU NOTES, BUT RATHER THAN COPY IT, MAKE IT YOUR OWN. THINK OF THIS AS A STARTING POINT.

Dear Name,

Thanks for taking the time to meet with me on (day). I enjoyed learning more about your company and the opportunities. I particularly liked (fill in the blank with specifics and/or personal observation). Thank you again for your consideration and I look forward to speaking with you again.

Sincerely,

Your Name
Email address
Phone number

While we're on the subject of professional communications, what does your voice mail say? If it's, "Hey, it's me, you know the drill," you need to change it, because it could be a deal breaker.

## THiS JOB SEARCH iS A FULL-TiME GiG iN iTSELF, BUT i NEED CASH. HOW DO i SQUEEZE iN A PART-TiME JOB?

It has been said that the more you do, the more you can do. I know this is true in my experience. And if you're trying to balance a check book while simultaneously kick starting a career, my bet is you also can identify. Making money and finding a career are two big projects.

It's amazing how quickly a job search can suck the time and energy out of a day. Consider it a lesson in time management and organization. If you have to work a part-time job in the balance, there really are no secrets. You have to just do it, and you have to make the most of it. That will likely mean late nights and a few missed parties.

The majority of my co-authors worked part-time jobs—everything from waiting tables to office jobs. This didn't surprise me. But what I found most interesting—and mildly disheartening— was they consistently said they invest less than 50 percent of their effort to their part-time jobs. Not even 50 percent! I have to say, this baffles me.

Sure, you might think, why put in the effort, it's just a part-time job. I'll put in the effort on my real job when I get it.

## BUT HERE'S THE PROBLEM

- Your work habits are just that—habits—and you're developing bad ones. It's never okay to slack off.

- You never know where that part-time job may lead. There are lots of people who started as clerks and ended up running the company.

- Your part-time boss may be your best reference when you're just starting out. Why squander that contact?

Yes, I am sure that scooping beans at Starbucks can be monotonous. On the other hand, I also know that the company not only puts employees through "coffee knowledge" classes to boost the quality of service they provide customers, but Starbucks also prides itself on internal hires. This tells me that every young person taking my order at the counter knows a thing or two about coffee beans and the roasting process. Well, there's a whole industry built around that! It also tells me that these so-called baristas perform consistently well and that they're liable to be looked upon favorably when a full-time assignment becomes available at headquarters or somewhere else in the field.

Earlier I suggested that you treat your first several jobs as stepping stones toward your ultimate career goals. Well, the same logic applies to part-time work. I think it's worth reframing the notion of "squeezing in" a part-time job to help you pocket cash and pay down debt. Fact is, the jobs also can help you pad your résumé. A part time job can teach:

Customer service

Cash management

Crisis management

Inventory

My bet is the responsibilities all have application to your long-term career goals. And in the long run as well as the short run, it's going to take a lot more than 50 percent of your effort to succeed.

# HOW DO i KNOW i'M GETTiNG A GOOD OFFER, AND HOW MUCH ROOM DO i HAVE TO NEGOTiATE?
A good offer is more than just the fact that you landed a great job, or in some cases a job, period. A great offer also has to be something you can live on. Chapter Eight, "I Don't Know Jack about Money," is devoted to questions about finances and budgeting. And although the topic may not rival a Foo Fighters' concert, please don't gloss over it because knowing what it will take for you to cover your monthly expenses is important when entertaining a new job offer.

Can you live on what they're offering to pay you? If not, that doesn't mean don't take the job. The job may be a critical stepping stone to your career and achieving your dream job. What it does mean is set up your life so you can afford to take the job.

When Jamie graduated college she knew she wanted to be in TV. Then she landed an internship in L.A. with one of the big entertainment companies. It paid zero but turned into a paid, full-time position. Great!, right? Wrong, the pay was $7 an hour, no benefits, no vacation. Night shift. Not exactly Hollywood glam. She could have blown off the job and waited for something better, but she took it, bit the bullet, bunked on a friend's couch, then later got an apartment with four other girls. She made ends meet because this job was key to her future and she knew it.

Once you know if you can live on the offer and if you're willing to make sacrifices for the job, then arm yourself with facts about how you should be compensated for the position. Consider spending some time clicking around the numerous salary tools online. (Just type "salary" into a search engine.) The sites can help you figure out what similar positions pay related to experience, and what benefits they typically include.

Also consider the demand for people like you. Is your field starving for young talent and the skills you possess? Or are there hundreds of others like you seeking similar opportunities? Hope for the former. Or do you have some specific skill, talent, or experience that makes you one of a kind. If you're an award-winning gymnast who has the strength to balance two people on your arms and one on your head, Cirque du Soleil will likely pay you big bucks. Or if you're like one of our Kansas State co-authors who was one of fewer than five people in the nation getting a degree in bakery science, you may find a baker's dozen or more bakeries vying for your talents.

But until you've spent time in your profession, those instances are rare and the list of things people have tried to negotiate is longer than my arm—everything from salary to time off to telecommuting privileges to parking spots. The bitter pill to swallow is that you really don't have much negotiating power when starting out. I guess this is the downside of being hired for potential. Once you have a few years' experience under your belt, your power to negotiate increases dramatically. Bookmark this page for when that time comes, so you remember to use the leverage that you will have.

If you feel uncomfortable negotiating with a new employer or boss, lots of people do, even people with years of experience. Some fear that making any requests will cause the offer to be

I WANT THE RIGHT JOB

# COMPARING JOB OPTIONS

This is a very useful tool that can help you weigh and prioritize all your options. Basically, it is an Excel spreadsheet into which you can condense all the information you have for the various jobs you are interviewing for. For many people, looking at the facts and feelings in this way will make the decision very clear. If you are one of them, go to the toolbox at www.NoMoreRamenOnline.com to download this template.

## TIER 1- PREFERRED COMPANIES, IDEAL POSITIONS, OR STRONG FINANCIAL SCENARIOS

| COMPANY NAME | INDUSTRY | POSITION/TITLE | TASKS- LIKES/DISLIKES | SALARY | BENEFITS | REVENUE/PROFIT | CONTACTS | CULTURE | ADDITIONAL COMMENTS |
|---|---|---|---|---|---|---|---|---|---|
| | | | | | | | | | COMPANY'S GROWTH PROSPECTS |
| | | | | | | | | | CAREER ADVANCE- MENT OPPORTUNITY |
| | | | | | | | | | REPUTATION |
| | | | | | | | | | WORKING ATMOS- PHERE AND ATTIRE |
| | | | | | | | | | QUALITY OF BOSS |
| | | | | | | | | | WORK AND VACATION SCHEDULE |
| | | | | | | | | | CONSISTENT WITH CAREER OBJECTIVES |

## TIER 2 - SOLID COMPANIES, GOOD OPPORTUNITIES TO GAIN EXPERIENCE, ADEQUATE FINANCIAL PACKAGES

| COMPANY NAME | INDUSTRY | POSITION/TITLE | TASKS- LIKES/DISLIKES | SALARY | BENEFITS | REVENUE/PROFIT | CONTACTS | CULTURE | ADDITIONAL COMMENTS |
|---|---|---|---|---|---|---|---|---|---|
| | | | | | | | | | |
| | | | | | | | | | |
| | | | | | | | | | |
| | | | | | | | | | |
| | | | | | | | | | |
| | | | | | | | | | |

## TIER 3 - JOBS AVAILABLE, COMPANIES HIRING, CONSIDERED A JOB, CASH FLOW OR PLACE-HOLDER

| COMPANY NAME | INDUSTRY | POSITION/TITLE | TASKS- LIKES/DISLIKES | SALARY | BENEFITS | REVENUE/PROFIT | CONTACTS | CULTURE | ADDITIONAL COMMENTS |
|---|---|---|---|---|---|---|---|---|---|
| | | | | | | | | | |
| | | | | | | | | | |
| | | | | | | | | | |
| | | | | | | | | | |
| | | | | | | | | | |
| | | | | | | | | | |

retracted. This is absolutely not true. In fact, some employers may even be disappointed if you don't show a little backbone—especially if you're being hired into a sales position, where negotiating skills are part of the job.

This is one of the few times that you'll be negotiating *with* the company rather than *for* the company. It's also where a little strategy can go a long way.

## JOB OFFER STRATEGIES

- **Control your excitement. Regardless of whether the offer exceeds your expectations, your best move is to appear even-keeled and objective.**

- **Respond to any offer with extreme graciousness, and ask for time to mull it over. (e.g., "Thank you very much. I appreciate your offer. Would you allow me a day to consider it?")**

- **Expect that the person making the offer also has scanned the salary sites and knows how the offer stacks up.**

- **Justify any requests for additional compensation with facts, such as salary survey information or superior benefits that you get in a current position.**

# WHAT ABOUT PUTTiNG OFF THE REAL WORLD?

A lot of people coming out of college are delaying the real world of working for a living. Do I think it is a good thing? Well, I probably won't be popular with this answer, but you didn't buy this book to hear just what you want to hear, I hope. No, I don't think it's a good thing. I think it's basically running away from yourself and things that make you uncomfortable.

Now, I have nothing against the person who takes a month off to backpack around Japan. If you've got the cash and can live comfortably with a toothbrush and three pairs of socks, you're better than me. When I was ready to see Japan I knew it wasn't going to be out of a backpack eating ramen noodles. It wasn't about the adventure; it was about seeing Japan.

But I do have a problem with the person who goes from year-long diversion to year-long diversion, hoping that sometime they will figure it all out. And of course, "it" is life. That's like saying, "I'm going to figure out college by staying nice and comfortable here in high school," or "I'm going to go to a different high school and, you know, experience that, but I'm sure I'll figure out college while I'm doing it." Give me a break.

Putting off the real world has consequences and you need to know that. Here are a few:

**OTHERS YOUR AGE WILL BE AHEAD OF YOU**: When it comes time to get a job, you may find yourself working for someone younger than you. Your friends may buy houses before you, they'll have cars before you, and they'll talk about their "real" lives before you.

**IT MAY NOT ADVANCE YOU**: Even though it's nice to think that spending a few years overseas sharing your time and talents will give you a leg up on others when it comes time to find a job, you may discover you are terribly wrong. While doing charity work is socially respected and admirable, don't be disappointed if it doesn't translate into a job when you return. It might, but it might not. Why? Because there will be people when you return, just as there were when you left, with real job experience that will probably get the job before you.

**IT MAY NOT BE CLARIFYING**: We talked with dozens of people who spent tons of time delaying their lives and are more baffled now than they were before. They are no closer to actually getting their life going than they were when they left.

**IT MAY MAKE YOU LESS HIRABLE**: When you're on an interview and the interviewer says, tell me about your work experience and you say that you spent the last year analyzing (a.k.a. "catchin'") the big waves in Hawaii and that's why you're qualified for the analyst's position. Well, your rank may drop just below the other 200 applicants who spent the last year as an analyst.

Sorry, just telling you the brutal facts.

Getting the right job can be more work than actually doing the job itself. You will have to do research. You will have to compromise. And in some cases you will want to quit before you even have a job to quit. But land that first job and the exhilaration will make it all worth it. You will be on the road to your future, facing it head on. Be confident, and just do it. You will grow and become more than you ever thought you could.

# RESOURCES

## THESE ARE SUGGESTED RESOURCES FROM BOTH 20-SOMETHINGS AND THE AUTHOR.

For a more complete list refer to Additional Resources (see page 228).

### CAREER ADVICE

www.TheVault.com

www.Jobhuntersbible.com

www.Seekingsuccess.com

www.careerjournal.com/jobhunting/change

### JOB SEARCH

www.Monster.com

www.hotjobs.com

www.careerbuilder.com

www.craigslist.com

I WANT THE RIGHT JOB

# 5

# i'M NOT PREPARED FOR A REAL JOB

"YOU ASK, HOW MUCH EFFORT AM I putting into my current job? Well, it's just part-time until I find something I really want to do, so I'd say, 10 percent. I know I should be giving it more, but it basically sucks and is really boring. Once I get my real job, I'll be more into it and give it more effort. Isn't that how it works?"

# i DO AND i UNDERSTAND.

Confucius says "I hear and I forget. I see and I remember. I do and I understand." Research from the United States Department of Health, Education, and Welfare suggests what this actually looks like in practice. They have found that learners retain information as follows:

- **10 percent of what they read**
- **20 percent of what they hear**
- **30 percent of what they see**
- **50 percent of what they see and hear**
- **70 percent of what they say**
- **90 percent of what they say and do**

See, however much it pains me to say so, I don't expect you'll remember everything you read in this book—not long term anyway. If I'm lucky, you'll remember a passage or two when you see them play out in your own life's experience. (A reminder for those times: I'm Nicholas Aretakis and you're reading *No More Ramen*.)

The fact is, your real learning and growth will come when you find yourself sidetracked for half the day by meetings, or when you find yourself chomping at the bit for more responsibility or when you get caught on the ugly side of some office politics. That's when you'll really come to master the workplace.

For now, take heart that beginning a new job is overwhelming for everyone. If it's not all the new names, it's the new processes, the new responsibilities, the new rules.

The first few days on the job are bound to make you feel greener than the state of Maine. Hold on, because you're going to learn more in a week on the job than you did in four (five . . . six . . . ) years of school.

# i'M STARTiNG A NEW JOB NEXT WEEK. ANY TiPS ON SETTLiNG iN?

The first day at a new job can easily feel like the first day of kindergarten. You know hardly anyone and every company treats your first day a little differently. To some companies, it's a non-event; at others they have a whole welcoming ritual with all kinds of bells and whistles! Regardless of the kind of company you joined, you can make the best of your first day. There's more to that first ten hours than figuring out where to park, where to sit, and filling out tax forms.

> In my very first real job, I was a PR writer. Every week I had five stories to research and write, and my main source was the marketing manager at our client company. My first week on the job, I knew what I had to get done and when, but the problem was my contact would never return my calls or get me the information I needed. So the second week, I got bold and called his boss to say I really needed a faster response. I guess you might call it being ripped a new one, because that's what I got when my contact called me to say, "Never again, ever, call my boss." I apologized, deleted his boss's number, and vowed it would never happen again. Here's the funny thing. My contact never missed another deadline. Did it help, yeah. But I learned to be way more diplomatic after that.

# BEiNG NEW ON THE JOB, HOW MUCH SHOULD i SPEAK UP iN MEETiNGS?

This is such a great question without an easy answer. In your first few jobs, it's easy to feel like you just have to go with the flow. You know, agree with your boss and go along with the crowd. That may be your personality or you may be suppressing the totally opinionated you! Well, here are some thoughts on first, second, or third jobs and speaking out.

# GETTING SETTLED IN A NEW JOB

### ORGANIZE YOUR WORKSPACE
That'll make you feel at home.

### MEET EVERYONE YOU CAN
It's as easy as "I don't believe we've met yet . . ."

### ASK LOTS OF QUESTIONS
Be a sponge and try to soak up as much as you can.

### START A READING PILE
Gather up everything you can about the products,
the company, the industry, etc.

### MEET WITH YOUR BOSS
Get your game plan together for the day, the week, the month, or longer.

### OBSERVE YOUR SURROUNDINGS
Take it all in and you'll gather clues to how it all works.

### LISTEN AND LEARN BEFORE YOU PRESENT ALL THE ANSWERS
Your simple solutions probably are neither simple nor solutions.

### ESTABLISH A ROUTINE FOR YOUR WORK WEEK
Look for patterns and go with the flow.

### FOLLOW THROUGH ON EVERYTHING YOU PROMISE
Be realistic and true to your word.

### REALIZE THAT THINGS TAKE TIME
It's good to be eager, but have some patience and be open,
outgoing, and results-oriented.

I think it is okay to speak out. In fact, most companies aren't hiring you to just go through the motions, they are hiring you to think. The key to speaking out is to do it diplomatically. I learned this lesson myself when I changed jobs the first time, many years ago now. Being a highly motivated young marketing manager with lofty goals, I set out with great ambition to achieve them. When our sales team met for quarterly reviews, I always spoke out, looking to demonstrate my leadership, even at the expense of those around me. Yeah, I got the promotion, but my overzealous behavior didn't win me any friends. When I became manager, I had a lot of relationship repairs to do.

That was a good lesson for me. I learned I could have done a lot more if I had been more diplomatic and patient. So if you're supposed to, speak out, but keep these guidelines in mind:

**ASK QUESTIONS FIRST:** Yes of course you want to prove how smart you are, but no one likes a person who thinks he knows everything and obviously doesn't. Giving answers without asking the questions first makes you look stupid.

**FRAME YOUR IDEAS IN THE FORM OF A QUESTION:** Instead of saying, "We need to call the company directly and tell them they need to pay right now," say, "Would it make sense to call the company directly and request payment?" That leaves room for discussion.

**WATCH YOUR TONE:** It's seldom a good idea to sound demanding, short, sarcastic, or anything other than gracious and inquiring. The example above pretty much says it all; you have to leave room for people to respond and not get defensive.

**IF YOU SEE A PROBLEM, OFFER A SOLUTION:** No one likes a person who points out all the reasons why something can't work. There are thousands of those for everything we see and do. If you see a problem, offer your comment in the form of a solution. For instance, "One way we might be able to overcome the design issue is to hire an expert," instead of "That won't work, there's no one here who can design that."

**DON'T GET DEFENSIVE:** If someone gives you attitude, sure you'll want to go right back at 'em, but you can't. You really can't, because then you lose, too. Let that person be the only one who makes the career-threatening move. Respond with genuine, not sarcastic, grace and you win.

**DON'T MAKE IT PERSONAL:** Business isn't personal, it's business, and that's the best way to think about it. Yes, be passionate about what you do, but don't let your emotions get the best of you in a work situation. Maintain rationality.

**DON'T WAIT:** When you have a real problem with a person or even how things are done at your work, speak up early. Recognize that the conflict isn't likely to just go away, so if you can talk about it before it becomes a big deal in your head, you'll find it easier to be cool and rational.

The bottom line to speaking out is do it, but do it properly. These guidelines should help. But know that every company culture and every job is different. So read the signs. If you get a positive response by speaking out, you work in an open culture. If you get glares, then your company may not be quite as open. Read the signs.

# i WAS A GREAT STUDENT iN SCHOOL, BUT iN THE JOBS i'VE HAD SiNCE THEN, i'M NOT SHiNiNG AS BRiGHTLY. ANY iDEAS?

School was one thing. Work in the real world is quite another. And the first thing you realize is that your ability to ace multiple choice tests like a pro doesn't translate to work. Unlike tests, the workplace is unpredictable and if you didn't develop the skills to go with the flow, then you probably aren't shining.

You're probably finding that at work, the instructions aren't so clear-cut and the end result is not quite as quantitative. For that reason, don't be surprised to find yourself busting your hump on a project, only to have it sidelined by another one at a moment's notice. Customers will change their minds. Other projects will flare up like brush fires and require immediate attention. Others you spent days or weeks working on will crash and burn, canceled due to "budget cuts." Your ability to succeed in such situations will be tied to your ability to change and adapt at a moment's notice, while continuing to deliver high-quality work.

Experts say that the key to flexibility, believe it or not, is a bit of rigidity in the form of disciplined time management. This is a skill that won't just help you be more flexible and more effective. It will improve your co-workers' perception of you, which is important, too. In Chapter Six, we'll get into a few tips about time management, but for now, know that it is fundamental to your success.

Beyond managing your time well so that you can be flexible, keep in mind that there's no room for C work on the job. Do poor work on the job and you'll be asked to do it again. And again. And again, until you get it right, which may involve late

# HOW TO MAKE
## YOUR PRESENTATiONS SHiNE

## VERBAL

Organize your thoughts on paper days before so you can sleep on it.

Figure out responses to possible questions in advance and practice them.

Decide how you'll handle questions,
either as you present or at the end of the presentation.

Be concise and succinct.

Keep visuals clean and exciting; use more images than bullets.

Show enthusiasm; after all you're on stage!

Practice, practice, practice.

## WRITTEN

Do an outline and sleep on it.

Write to your audience in plain language, not business-speak.

Keep it brief but complete, with short paragraphs.

Use charts and graphs to help get your point across.

Format for easy reading and printing, with lots of sub headings.

One more thing . . . be observant.
Look for interesting presentations and then pattern yours off of those.
What's boring to you is probably boring to many.

nights and weekends—without extra pay. Inevitably it may also lead to less exciting projects and really hold you back in your career. In the workplace, A work is about more than getting things done on time with no major misspellings. It's about bringing inspiration and excellence to your work, whether written or spoken.

With quality a given, shining on the job is also about jumping in. What's that mean? Well, simply, if you want to really stand out, which is what it takes to advance, you need to be the one who asks, "What else can I do?" If your boss is bogged down on a project, say, "Let me help." If you complete an assignment, don't just surf your favorite blogs until your boss gives you something else to do. Instead, ask for more work. That alone will set you apart.

And did I mention that your willingness to do whatever, whenever with A-quality has to happen 100 percent of the time? It does. You no longer have the liberty of turning your effort on and off based on your own set of standards or the hangover you're nursing from the party the night before. There are no class audits and no pass/fail courses that you can skate through. Everything is make or break. So my last point is that if you want to shine on the job, assume a new attitude of excellence 100 percent of the time. After all, people are counting on you—your boss, your customers, your co-workers—so deliver daily.

# CLASSIC WORK HOURS ARE 8 AM TO 5 PM. WHAT HOURS ARE PEOPLE REALLY WORKING?

They say we live in a global economy, and the last time I looked at the globe, I saw time zones. Lots of them. On my phone I have a program that shows me which part of the world is in daylight and which part isn't at any given moment. Aside from it being a cool program that keeps me on track when I'm traveling, it just brings to light that work is constant in our global economy, and work is happening and amassing from the moment you wake up. Work can be constant if we want it to be, and increasingly, staying competitive doesn't give any of us much choice. The Bureau of Labor Statistics data shows that the 40-hour workweek has been in steady decline since John Travolta was a Sweathog (that's the 70s) and the 49-hour plus work week has been on the increase. Breaks are practically nonexistent. I know one guy who says to the person on the line he's in "the library" when he's taking a call in the bathroom. I guess nothing is sacred.

Sure you can work nine to five, but keeping banker's hours— though bankers will tell you that they don't even keep those hours anymore—will not get you very far. Why? Because things come up. An email may come through at 4 pm for a 5 pm meeting so you can pull a presentation together for a 9 am meeting the next day. Do you really want to be the one to say, "I can't go, I've got a girls' night out tonight," or "Count me out, there's a new episode of *The Apprentice* on tonight"? That's what weekends and TiVo are for. Adapting is a big part of succeeding, and *The Apprentice* is a sacrifice worth making if you are hungry enough.

Regardless of what your company's published hours are, plan on working until your job is done, and done right. Sometimes that means weekends. Sometimes holidays. Most full-time jobs don't pay overtime, either, so don't expect to pad your wallet.

Beyond what's required of you, another thing to consider is your status on the organizational chart. Most people start at the bottom, but I'm sure you don't want to stay there long. Logging some extra time could be one way to push the status quo and impress upon your managers that you're serious about the job and that you are willing to put in the work that's necessary to excel. This is one way you can use the clock to your advantage.

Aim to get to the office on time in the morning, even early if you have a lot of work to get done. And if you have to stay late, well, that goes with the territory, too, sometimes. It's not just about logging the hours. The last thing you want to do is kill time surfing the Internet just so you can look like you are staying late and being a hero. The important thing is to be productive during the hours you are on the job. Results speak loudly. If you're spending extra hours on the job, be sure you have the completed work to show for it, or the message will surely be either you are inefficient or just screwing off.

## EVERYONE AT MY JOB CONSTANTLY COMPLAINS ABOUT WORK, THE COMPANY, AND OUR BOSS. IS IT LIKE THAT EVERYWHERE?

If you've ever watched *Saturday Night Live,* you may have caught a sketch written around a character named "Debbie Downer." As the name suggests, the character just sucks the fun out of every situation they put her in—whether a birthday party or a Disney vacation. There's no shortage of people who do the same thing, every day, in corporate America and even nonprofit America.

The *Saturday Night Live* sketch brings to mind a business leadership presentation I once attended. The speaker posed a question that I thought to be right on: Do you bring more energy to a room when you walk in or when you walk out?

It's a litmus test for the Debbie Downer in each of us.

Unfortunately, you're going to encounter people on the job who just complain incessantly. Maybe they're miserable and nothing will satisfy them? Regardless, I suggest you distance yourself

# HOW SATiSFiED ARE
## PEOPLE iN THEiR JOBS?

**A RECENT HARRIS INTERACTIVE SURVEY\***
**UNCOVERED THE FOLLOWING STATISTICS**
**ON AMERICAN JOB SATISFACTION.**

Across America, 45 percent of workers say they
are either satisfied or extremely satisfied with their jobs.

Only 20 percent feel very passionate about their jobs.

33 percent believe they have reached a dead-end in their career.

21 percent are eager to change careers.

Older workers are the most satisfied
and the most engaged in their work.

Younger workers are the most distressed and they feel
the least amount of loyalty to their employers.

Small firm employees feel far more engaged
in their work than their big corporate counterparts.

Job security, health-care coverage, and professional development
are valued above additional compensation.

\*The New Employee/Employer Equation Survey was conducted
by Harris Interactive, Inc., a leading market research firm,
and included responses from a nationwide sample of
7,718 American employees 18 and over.

Let us know how satisfied you are at
www.NoMoreRamenOnline.com.

from these people—take their complaints with a grain of salt and do not join the bandwagon. Complaining leads to procrastinating, which leads to missed deadlines, which leads to poor performance. Complaining about a particular situation instead of recommending a solution or alternative approach is counterproductive. Don't point out problems; pose solutions to problems. Besides, your own complaints, made public, are ripe for the rumor mill and can only end up making you look bad.

On the other hand, enthusiasm is infectious. If you take on a job, be optimistic about the prospects and the value of its completion. By contributing a good attitude, there is a better chance that you'll motivate others to have a good attitude, and that will yield a higher probability for success. Not just that, but people will enjoy working with you and invite you to collaborate on other projects. You will emerge as a leader. And leaders get promoted.

# WHAT'S WiTH ALL THE MEETiNGS? AND HOW DO i GET MY WORK DONE AROUND THEM?

You will undoubtedly spend a lot of time in meetings over your career. There will be brainstorming sessions, meetings with customers, training seminars, and performance reviews. You will have meetings to determine which meetings you should attend, and meetings to reduce the number of meetings you have. It can seem ridiculous, I know. Unfortunately, the list is not getting shorter any time soon. You're just going to have to get used to the fact that meetings are an element—and sometimes a necessary evil—of the working world.

Balancing meetings with your "real" work can be an art form, sometimes. In fact, this is why many people end up working such long hours. They spend standard business hours running between meetings and are left pulling double duty just to get their deliverables in on schedule. Again, it's just a reality of the modern workplace.

In light of this reality, the savior for many people becomes solid time management skills. Numerous books and other resources can help you in this regard. (Also see Chapter Six.) For starters, I suggest you always carry your daily "to-do" list along with you, with priority items indicated. Force yourself to chip away at your to-do list during every free moment you have, before, after, and in between meetings.

Sometimes you may find it's more efficient to knock out some of the less critical activities first, especially if it won't take a large amount of your time to do them. Also, try to carve out specific times of the day to manage and respond to emails and voice mails—two of the biggest time suckers in a day—after meetings.

Another tool for managing a meeting-heavy schedule is to make sure meeting time is as effective as possible. The sooner you learn how to prepare, attend, and run effective meetings, the better off you and your colleagues will be. The box on the next page offers some guidelines for running and participating in meetings.

## MY JOB iS KiND OF EASY. HOW DO i KEEP MY DAYS AND MY WORK EXCiTiNG?

If you ever set out to lose weight—even five pounds—you know from experience that progress doesn't always happen as quickly as you want it to. I know that doing the same tasks over and over— 30 minutes on the treadmill, 50 laps in the pool—can become dull. But you have the power to not let those critical tasks or your job become robotic. And whether it's losing 30 pounds or making partner by 30, it starts with staying focused on your goals and objectives.

# MEETiNG ROLES AND RESPONSiBiLiTiES

**IF YOU FIND YOURSELF INVOLVED IN A MEETING, EITHER ATTENDING IT OR RUNNING IT, HERE ARE SOME POINTERS THAT WILL MAKE SURE YOU GET THE MOST OUT OF EVERY MINUTE AND LOOK GOOD IN THE PROCESS.**

## MEETING CHAIRPERSON

Clearly define the purpose and goals of the meeting.

Create an agenda.

Identify who should be there, and whose presence is not essential. (Too many participants in a meeting can prove counter-productive.)

Arrange dial-in numbers for individuals conferencing in.

Establish meeting protocol (e.g., no cell phones, one person speaks at a time).

Ensure meetings begin and end on time.

Publish action items within 24 hours of the meeting's end.

Follow up as required.

## MEETING ATTENDEES

Arrive on time and prepared.

Contribute to the discussion, but don't dominate (i.e., pause between sentences, permitting others to interject questions and comments).

Stay focused; leave tangential conversations for another time.

Complete assigned action items in a timely manner.

We know that getting ahead isn't easy. If goals were one day affairs, they'd be called activities. The problem is people tend to let themselves become too comfortable in their jobs. They lose track of their goals and forget what it's like to be challenged. They become complacent, decide to settle for mediocrity, and conclude that work is inherently boring.

Buck the trend. If you find yourself feeling that your job is too easy, ask yourself if it's because you have become too comfortable in your day-to-day assignment. If that's the case, there's only one thing to do: ask for new challenges. Remind your manager (or your manager's manager) of your goals, reinforce your desire to advance along that route, and ask if you can be doing more to get there. It sounds simple because it is.

No one that I know has lost a job because they asked for more to do. But they have been promoted.

> I know a guy who works for JP Morgan/Chase.
> He was bored in his entry-level data-entry job and came to me because he wanted to quit and look for a job in marketing.
> Now meet him today. He's still at JP Morgan/Chase. He loves his marketing job and is heading toward his ultimate career goal.
> How'd he do it? By talking to a supervisor in the company, communicating his goals, and asking for a more challenging position. Lapsed time? Two weeks.
> Did I mention the pay raise?

# HOW DO i PRiORiTiZE AND BALANCE MY PERSONAL OBJECTiVES WiTH MY PROFESSiONAL OBJECTiVES?

Of course, there's one caveat to asking for more work: odds are you're going to get it. That means not only are you committing yourself to doing more things, but also to doing more things well. Taking responsibility and delivering on your promises is fundamental to success in business. This means no shortcuts. But on the up side, it also means you're going to learn more, experience more, and get to do more cool things. Your days will go by at lightning speed.

In the focus groups, my co-authors graded themselves as 85 percent reliable. Many said they often looked for shortcuts—great if it's in the interest of productivity and doesn't compromise quality, but often times, this isn't the case.

Shortcuts typically are just opportunities to quickly mark things off a to-do list. They speak of laziness. And I promise you that if you get into the habit of taking shortcuts, and the shortcuts result in work that is sub-par, you will limit your advancement. You also will meet more resistance the next time you ask for new challenges.

Remember, life is truly what you make of it. Though a job may seem easy, you can always work harder, work smarter, and contribute. Demonstrate that you are a hard worker, committed, and an overachiever, and you'll be rewarded for your efforts.

The world is distracted, but not blind. Cream does eventually rise to the top.

# i REALLY CAN'T STAND <iNSERT NAME>, AND THE FEELiNG SEEMS MUTUAL, BUT i HAVE TO WORK WiTH THiS PERSON. HOW DO i HANDLE THE SiTUATiON?

While you will learn countless new things upon entering the real world, there's at least one thing you already know: everyone is not going to be your friend.

If you're anything like me, through school and your extracurricular activities you always wanted to be liked and have friends. It's different at work. Starting up a new job, you will find that people are not often cut from similar molds. They have varying backgrounds, varying educations, varying opinions, ideas, and objectives. I always have found it best to be cautious in developing professional relationships. It's best to err on the conservative side.

I suggest you establish a work persona. Refrain from letting co-workers know too much too soon about your personal life. The last thing you need is to work extremely hard, make solid strides toward a promotion, and then have someone turn one of your extracurricular activities against you. (e.g., "Tim is a great salesman, but did you know he's also a fantasy football fanatic. I wonder if his constant analysis of football statistics and his football-game-laden weekends will distract him from making his quarterly goals.") The reality is there may be no problem, but it's perception that counts. And this is another reality: people always look out for themselves, first. And some have no problem making others look bad if it means they'll wind up smelling like roses.

If you're in a situation where you and a colleague just don't see eye to eye, always take the high road. Try your best to be professional.

That means debating without being disagreeable, taking nothing personally, never holding a grudge, and always maintaining your composure. Your ability to be assertive while at the same time kind, open-minded, and humble will take you far.

If the situation keeps deteriorating and your manager can't help, you may have to evaluate options for transferring to another department or finding another job altogether. Whatever happens, do not get combative or create a situation where you are leaving on bad terms. That could wind up hurting you down the road.

# WHAT'S THE WORD ON BUSINESS TRAVEL?

No doubt, the biggest up side to any job that involves travel is the opportunity to see the world. I've visited Australia, Asia, Europe, and cities throughout the United States all on the company dime. Many times I flew business class and stayed in top hotels. Along the way, I snorkeled with sea turtles in the Great Barrier Reef, I hiked through tropical rainforests in Thailand, and I jogged down the Champs de Elysees.

Yes, traveling has been a highlight of my career. Many of the trips I have made would not have been possible for me if business hadn't been the main reason. Truth is, I could fill another book with stories from my traveling experiences, and business travel can be fun, social, and even glamorous. But what I want to focus on here are the responsibilities that come with it. Because it's not all about pub crawling and oxygen bars.

The main thing to consider when you travel on business is that you are essentially an ambassador for your employer. Your actions will reflect not just on you, but also on the firm that's paying you to be there. Interacting with clients over the phone is one thing, but when you're sitting face to face with them on their turf or at a conference, you better darn well look and act the part.

This is about professionalism. It means you're on time and prepared for every appointment. It means you dress professionally, and if you are not sure what that means, you ask your boss. It means you smile and display enthusiasm even though your plane sat delayed on the tarmac for two hours. It means you exercise impeccable table manners, and, when alcohol is flowing, you practice moderation.

# RULES FOR THE ROAD

**BE SOCIABLE.**
Don't get sloshed.

**RENT A CAR.**
Don't rent a sports car.

**BOOK AN AISLE.**
Give up the aisle if your boss has a middle.

**SET AN ALARM.**
Set two alarms and arrange for a wake-up call.

**BUILD RELATIONSHIPS.**
Don't spill your guts.

**LOOK SHARP.**
Learn how to iron.

Travel also is not an excuse for slacking on your responsibilities. Why not make good use of your time on the plane? Bring a laptop or PDA and catch up on emails, practice your presentation, or write up that report. And when you show up at that luxury hotel or even the budget motor inn, remember that deadlines are deadlines, and as much as you may want to take a wind-surfing lesson while on business in Maui, when work calls, you need to answer. Otherwise, you risk not enjoying the privilege of business travel for very much longer.

Finally, think about the people with whom you are traveling and the timetable you are working on. If the trip is a short one, try to pack everything you need in carry-on luggage. Waiting at baggage claim takes time and it may be the difference between being on time to an appointment or being late if your plane was delayed. If you can get by without that extra pair of shoes, why pack them? It's just more to put away when you return.

# HOW MUCH FUN iS TOO MUCH FUN TO HAVE WiTH THE PEOPLE AT WORK?

Some companies out there work hard and they play hard—and they're proud of it. They can be very demanding, but are also a lot of fun to work for. They are also the companies that can give you just enough rope to hang yourself. True story: I know a person who worked for one of these companies. They'd hold huge parties, alcohol would flow, and everyone would let out a ton a steam built up from really long hours and a lot of pressure. At one of those events a colleague got a little out of hand and the ensuing sexual harassment lawsuit was devastating to all involved. Too much rope, floor drops out, hung!

These stories and worse happen all the time to both men and women. One person I know has a snapshot of a guy he works with who was caught passed out on a bench in a hotel lobby during a company convention. So again, be cool about parties and alcohol. Especially now that your less-than-shining moment can be captured forever by anyone's picture phone or PDA— even videotaped for all of posterity!

But just as your physical behavior can get you busted, you're mouth can hang you, too. Even if you're out partying with a few people from your department, just assume that anything you say can and will come back to haunt you. So probably saying things like how big your boss's butt is isn't a good idea, no matter how many laughs you'd get. Enough said?

## WHAT'S PROPER ETIQUETTE iN THE CUBE FARM?
Many rules of the workplace are clearly spelled out for you when you start a new job: the type of clothes you're expected to wear; the hours you're expected to keep; the way you should answer the phone. These things vary from company to company, but most of the time, they are givens.

Proper etiquette in a cubicle environment, on the other hand, is not always addressed in the employee handbook. Often the rules are unspoken. This is a shame, I think, because in such close quarters, even the smallest disruptions can ruin productivity.

We've all seen the impromptu meeting on the floor. Two colleagues encounter one another in passing and suddenly strike up a five-minute conversation. Great if they're tackling hot-button issues, but pity the person sitting on the other side of that thin cubicle wall who also is working against a deadline.

I give kudos to the person in that situation who speaks up, asking the two to move their conversation elsewhere. But sometimes it's not so easy. Maybe one of the two is the boss, or maybe there's fear of ruffling feathers. Best bet is to not put your colleagues in that situation.

If you find yourself and a colleague in an extended conversation while others in the immediate vicinity are trying to work,

exercise common decency and move to the water cooler or
some other more acceptable meeting place.

## COMMON DECENCY IS REALLY WHAT CUBE ETIQUETTE BOILS DOWN TO

- Control the volume of your voice; I'm not talking library whispers, but it's not a party, either.

- Keep personal phone calls brief, better still if you can make the calls from the break room, using your cell phone.

- Keep your cell phone ring-tone volume low or on vibrate; does the person in the next cube really want to hear Eric Cartman saying "You will respect my authoritah!" every time your phone rings?

- Don't eavesdrop; at least, don't contribute to other people's conversations.

- Dispose of food containers in the break room; no one wants to spend the afternoon inhaling wafts of your discarded Kung Pao Chicken lunch special.

- Use discretion with your cubicle décor.

# HOW DOES WRITING A BUSINESS EMAIL DIFFER FROM WRITING A PERSONAL EMAIL?

Some of the most treasured and scrutinized documents from political leaders are the letters they exchange with other dignitaries and notable political figures. The letters often convey the stories behind the stories that we read in the newspapers—you know, the subplots. As presidential historians will attest, the letters also often drip with courtesy and compliments. And there's no mistaking why. The letters become part of the written history, part of the public record.

I'M NOT PREPARED FOR A REAL JOB

So what would it say about a leader to have one of those letters fraught with spelling errors and poor grammar, let alone nasty remarks?

Email is no doubt one of the most transformative business tools to have emerged in the past decade. And there's a lesson about writing business emails to be learned from presidential letters. The way you write speaks just as loudly about your character as does what you say. Ask yourself, "Would I be proud or morti-fied if an email that I wrote and sent landed on the front page of *USA Today* or *The New York Times*? My advice is only write emails you'd be proud of. There is very little that can't be handled diplomatically.

Writing in all lowercase, using poor grammar or instant mes-saging abbreviations, and misspelling words are big no's. Think about the message these things say. (Hint: lazy; not concerned with appearance, immature.) If you must commit one or more of these crimes of the pen, do so in your personal emails and cell phone text messages. For business communications—email and otherwise—you're best off adhering to convention.

Among other things, that means using a salutation (e.g., "Dear Amanda"), limiting abbreviations, and always, always, always running spell-check before pushing the send button. For any email, include a digital signature with your address, phone, fax, and website. That's a great courtesy and a time saver for every-one involved.

Now, what about using your work email as your personal email? In theory, it sounds like no big deal and seems like a time-saving idea. After all, it will take you more time to check your personal emails if you have to go to Yahoo or Hotmail or some-where else. Well, save yourself time by checking your personal emails at home and keep your work email strictly business. Yes, that will help you manage your time, but it could also save you your job and even, in extreme situations, keep you out of jail. Realize that email archives are company property and in the event of any kind of lawsuit or court proceeding, all emails are fair game for review.

Everything, including that email stating how much you can't stand your boss or the one relating in detail the events of a wild Friday night, are not for company email systems. Your words in all their glory could end up on the front page of *The New York Times,* either now or 20 years from now when you're being confirmed for your appointment as secretary of state. It can happen! Ask ousted FEMA director Michael Brown. News headlines reported that on the day that Hurricane Katrina hit the Gulf Coast, Brown found time to email an aide after an appearance on TV. He wrote, "I am a fashion god." His aide, Cindy Taylor, replied, "You look fabulous—and I'm not talking the makeup!" Then, in reference to his tie, Brown replied, "I got it at Nordstrom's . . . Are you proud of me? Can I quit now? Can I go home?" Not good.

Not only does this prove that we all should watch what we email and to whom we email, know that just because you delete emails doesn't mean they go away. They absolutely don't. Your emails reside in back-up anywhere and everywhere. On your recipient's computer. On network back-ups at work. On the receiving company's back-ups. In the archives of heaven only knows how many places. So if you get personal in email, even with a workmate, know that there is no such thing as privacy.

And all this goes for phone records, too, particularly if you have a company cell phone. Recognize that your company gets your phone bills and all records are available for review by anyone. (Probably not a good idea to call 900 numbers on your cell phone.)

I'M NOT PREPARED FOR A REAL JOB

# NOW THAT i HAVE A REAL JOB, iS THERE ANYTHiNG i SHOULD KNOW ABOUT SOUNDiNG PROFESSiONAL ON THE PHONE?

Good phone communication is arguably more important than any other form of communication, particularly in business. Why? Because the phone call is often the first encounter you have with other people. Make sure your phone manner delivers a great first impression. Follow these rules and you'll have no problem.

**ANSWER THE PHONE ON THE FIRST OR SECOND RING**: Be sure to answer as quickly as you can. Everyone is busy and a quick answer saves time, plus it's common courtesy.

**SMILE WHEN YOU ARE TALKING**: This will ensure you sound pleasant and welcoming to the caller. There's nothing worse than a gruff phone manner.

**SPEAK CLEARLY**: Phone receivers are notorious for bad audio quality, so be sure you enunciate your letters and do the "P as in Paul" routine when spelling names or emails as needed.

**BE IN THE MOMENT**: Pay attention to the call. Distractions can lead to a disjointed conversation, and the excessive "uhs" and "ums" while you struggle to gather your thoughts will make you sound unprofessional.

**THANK THE CALLER FOR HOLDING**: If you must put some-one on hold, instead of saying, "Sorry about that" when you return, say, "Thank you for holding." It sounds better and is more positive.

**KEEP HOLD TIMES TO NO LONGER THAN 30 SECONDS**: If you must keep someone on hold for longer, return to the caller and say, "It'll be a few moments longer, would you like to continue to hold, or can I call you back?"

**HAVE A PAD AND PEN READY:** Answer the phone ready to take down notes, even just a phone number. That way you won't inconvenience the caller by wasting time searching for something to write with and you won't miss a detail.

## RULES FOR LEAVING VOICE MAIL MESSAGES

- Keep them brief, no five-minute messages: Most voice mail messages can be 30 seconds or less. They get longer because people find it hard to wrap up the message, so they keep repeating themselves, looking for an end. Short and sweet: "Hi, this is Jane Doe with the ABC Company. I'm calling to confirm the location for our meeting. Please call me back at 490.555.1212, that's 490.555.1212. Thanks."

- Leave your full name, company, and the reason for your call: This is really all you need in a voice mail message. Keep it simple, short, and clear.

- Say your phone number slowly: And repeat it. There's nothing worse than a long message you have to play over and over again because the caller left her phone number so quickly that even Einstein wouldn't have been able to compute the numbers, let alone write them down.

- Leave date and time: Although some phones announce this automatically, many don't and it's nice to know when the message was left.

- Be persistent but not a pest: Sometimes it will take repeated calls to get through to someone. Be understanding when you call by saying things like, "I know you are busy but . . ." or "I'll only take a few minutes of your time." Avoid "I've left you three messages and you haven't called me back!" Be nice and if necessary go through an assistant or other colleague, never over the person's head. No snitching.

# "WHO SAiD THAT?" EFFECTiVE CONFERENCE-CALLiNG

WITH TODAY'S GLOBAL ECONOMY, CHANCES ARE
GOOD YOU WILL HAVE TO PARTICIPATE IN A CONFERENCE
CALL EVERY NOW AND THEN—OR ALL THE TIME.
IT'S A UNIQUE KIND OF MEETING, WHEN YOU ARE
INTERFACING WITH A GROUP OF PEOPLE, AND
THE ONLY CONTEXT CLUES YOU HAVE ARE AUDIO.
HERE ARE A FEW TIPS TO MAKE SURE YOUR MESSAGE
COMES THROUGH LOUD AND CLEAR.

You may be great at recognizing voices,
but not every one is. Identify yourself when you begin speaking.
"This is Charles, and I think . . ."

Wait your turn—you might have a really good point to make,
but don't speak while someone else has the floor.
Your turn will come along in just a minute.

You asked for the call—be the leader. Just like any meeting,
conference calls need an agenda and someone to monitor the meeting.
It's a good idea to email the agenda ahead of time so everyone comes prepared.
Then during the meeting prompt the participants to continue and take turns.
"Sandra, do you have anything to add?"

Take the call in a quiet space. At the very least close your door, or if you are in a
cubicle, go into a private office or a conference room. Keep paper rustling and
pencil tapping to a minimum. If you are taking notes on your computer, be sure
you make that known so none of the participants thinks you are multi-tasking
and not paying attention. Remember, the only clues they have are audio.

Conference calling can be a quick, efficient way to touch base on a subject even
though the participants are remote from one another. It's just another sign
that the world is shrinking, and how amazing that is.

## AND THEN A FEW COMMON-SENSE RULES

- Make sure your cell phone is off before you add any colorful editorial comments about the person you were speaking with. How many times have you heard horror stories about people who let the expletives fly only to find out the phone was still on. Oops!

- Be sure your cell phone, if you use it for work, is as professional as your desk phone. Can the "Hey this is Mike . . . you know what to do (beep)" stuff.

- Return calls as soon as possible, but certainly within the same day—even if it means doing your "real work" after hours. That's kind of life in the work world.

I can summarize all these rules into one you've probably heard before: "Do unto others . . . ." Yes, that applies here, too.

# i WANTED TO TAKE OFF AROUND LABOR DAY AND MY VACATiON WAS REFUSED. THAT iS SO UNFAiR.

As much as most companies would like to grant you time off when you request it, sometimes demands of the job make it impossible to do so. Rather than think the situation unfair, take a look at the circumstances. It may be that your boss is being unreasonable, but more often there are legitimate reasons.

## HERE ARE A FEW EXAMPLES

- You might have had time off around a few other holidays and it was time for someone else in your department to have a break.

- There might be a big project that needs to get done and the day you requested just wasn't possible given the workload.

- You may have already used your allotment of vacation days.

- Your boss didn't have enough notice and had committed to her supervisors that work would be done; she needs you there.

One of the most important qualities you can build within yourself is empathy. That means you understand the position others are in. When asking for time off, it helps if you can empathize with those around you and balance your desire for time off with the needs and commitments of others.

Beyond that, there's the whole idea of being a team player. If it is always all about you when it comes to vacations or even little things like taking breaks on your clock, not your team's, then life at work isn't going to be very fun for you or for those around you. Flexibility is key.

## I'M SICK OF ALL THIS GRUNT WORK. I COULD MAKE MORE MONEY WAITING TABLES. SHOULD I QUIT?

Here again, I raise the question of your goals. While working a restaurant job or some other role in a service industry can be lucrative, you have to ask yourself how it fits into your grand plan.

If, say, you envision a career in hotel and restaurant management or restaurant public relations, then hey, waiting tables for a while may not be such a bad move. It'll give you a practical base of experience to draw from. But if your plan has more to do with finance than fajitas, the restaurant job likely isn't your best option.

Face it, you're going to have to do the grunt work when you're just starting out. There's no getting around it. That comes with being on the lowest rung of the ladder, and it's how we all learned the ropes of our business. At large accounting firms, that means you're the one who will be scrutinizing clients' books on New Year's Eve. At a magazine publisher, you'll be the one fact-checking stories while the more senior staff are sipping wine at press lunches.

Stick it out. Be open to where the grunt work may lead you, particularly if it's consistent with your long-term goals. Jamie from the last chapter is a good example. She knew she wanted to be in the entertainment business and willingly worked the night shift in the tape file room for less money than what she could have earned flipping burgers. And she did it for two years. Today, just three years out of college, she's a producer for one of the top entertainment shows on TV and is on the red carpet at the Oscars, the Emmy awards, and every other Hollywood happening. All the grunt work was worth it to Jamie.

Also remember that it's easier to find work that you'll enjoy when you already have work to begin with. Not only will you appear more in demand to employers, but you also won't have to worry about where the next rent check is coming from. That'll keep you from taking the wrong job and perpetuating your position on the bottom rung.

# HOW MANY JOB HOPS ARE TOO MANY?

Throughout your career, you will always be able to find reasons why you should jump from one job to another. It may be a money play—getting paid more to do similar work for another employer. You may not particularly like your boss or the people you work with. You may not feel excited about the customer base or product area you support. Or you may simply be bored with your job responsibilities.

While it's becoming increasingly more common to hop from job to job early in your career, I suggest you avoid falling prey to the temptation too often. Think about how your résumé will look if it's checkered with a series of jobs that each lasted less than a year. Prospective employers may question your judgment about the employers you select or even worse, infer that you lack sufficient patience or maturity to stick with a job. Or they may question your commitment to work and whether it's worth investing money to train you.

There's no set rule on how long you should stay at one particular job or how many job hops are too many. The question only emphasizes the benefits to be gained from selecting the right company from the outset. Use your best judgment. Unless there are unusual circumstances at play, try to commit to jobs for at least two years. The stability will work to your benefit— you'll learn more, your responsibilities will increase, and you'll likely get a raise. These are all things that look good to future employers.

Bottom line, don't job hop to the point where questions of loyalty will hamper your prospects when you're competing for a great job at the next Google.

# HOW CAN i MAKE SURE MY CURRENT EMPLOYER WiLL BE WiLLiNG TO SERVE AS A REFERENCE DOWN THE ROAD?

In the sporting world, the way you start a competition often can mean the difference between winning and losing. But as you know, the sports pages don't pay much attention to kickoffs. It's the results that matter—the final whistle, the finish line. Let's face it, the final score is what counts.

Similarly, the way you terminate a job often colors the way you are remembered by your managers and colleagues. Do it right and you should have no doubt that they'll be willing to sing praises on your behalf.

First and foremost, consider your performance on the job. Did you do good quality work consistently and deliver results? If you were your manager, would you be sorry to see you go? That's really the biggest factor when thinking about the kind of reference a current employer could give on your behalf. If you performed on the job and made life easier for those around you, odds are you can count on your managers for glowing references.

Let's assume that's the case—that your performance is not a question. Securing the reference then becomes a matter of exit strategy, and there's a lot to be said for finishing gracefully. Equally important, don't leave them high and dry. You want to give as much notice of your departure as possible to allow your employer to plan for things after you leave. Whether you're leaving for a new job or to go back to school or for some other reason, make sure you give at least two weeks' notice. There's no better way to spoil a reputation than to drop the bomb that you're leaving and then run.

With that in mind, once you've given notice, make every effort to close all loops on the work that's currently on your plate. Try to leave nothing hanging, and make clear where colleagues will be able to find any important files you created after you've gone. You may even consider leaving them with your contact information so they can get your help with any questions that arise.

Along with these actions, leave the right impression with your words. Regardless of how true it is, emphasize that the experience was positive. Make it known that you value the time you spent working there, as well as any training and guidance you received.

At that point, the only thing left to do will be to ask for the reference. Just as you made your goals known to your managers so they could help you pursue them, you also want to make known your intention to use them as references. If you've made their lives easier while working for them, they'll tell you it's the least they can do.

I have always kept in touch with the managers I've worked for. They have provided years' worth of references and we have become part of each other's network helping each other out whenever we can.

Clearly, the real world is, well, real, and if you have one, two, or more real jobs under your belt, you're finding out that there are no practices for the real thing. This is it. If you have found that hard to cope with and have found yourself either losing interest in your job or being let go from your job, the only thing you can do is assess why and make the necessary changes. The recommendations in this chapter are based on the facts, and sometimes the facts are not easy to swallow. You probably didn't love everything you read in this chapter. Sorry about that, but as you are rapidly discovering, every day is a day of discovery and a day of adjustment. If nothing else it keeps life interesting.

# RESOURCES

## THESE ARE SUGGESTED RESOURCES FROM BOTH 20-SOMETHINGS AND THE AUTHOR.

For a more complete list refer to Additional Resources
(see page 228).

**www.about.com/careers**

**www.quintcareers.com**

**www.careersurf.com**

# 6

# I'M NOT GETTING AHEAD, HELP!

"IT TOOK ME A FEW YEARS TO FIGURE out I wanted to go into design. I spent a year at an ad agency in account services and that wasn't at all for me. Then it took almost a year to figure something else out. Now with all that time lost—like two years—I feel like I'm really behind where I should be. The only jobs I'm finding in the field I want to go into are way entry level. It's like I'm starting all over again."

# iF ONLY iT WERE A MONTAGE . . . Go to the

movies enough and you tend to notice patterns in the way Hollywood tells stories.

There are common plot lines: boy meets girl, boy and girl fall in love, boy loses girl, and boy and girl get back together again.

There's also the frequent use of the montage—the music video within the movie, where the soundtrack fills the absence of dialogue and a sequence of scenes propel you through time as the main character does his or her thing. Think about the scene in *Napoleon Dynamite* when Napoleon is learning and then perfecting his dance routine.

Wouldn't it be great if your career could move that quickly? Load your favorite .mp3 and arrive at your breakthrough moment by the time the song ends? Well, as you know, it just doesn't work that way.

If I were to make a montage of my own experience, I'd have to condense about ten years—years!—of stress over last-minute deadlines, 60-hour weeks, and incremental promotions to get to the point where I was finally beginning to thrive. And it happened a lot faster for me than it does for most others.

If you want an office with a door and executive travel perks and BMW bonuses, you definitely have the power to get them. But temper your expectations. It's going to take longer than a montage music video to get there.

# i ALREADY FEEL LiKE i'M NOT AS FAR ALONG AS i SHOULD BE. iS THAT COMMON?

If you already feel like you're not yet where you want to be professionally, I have good news for you: you're far ahead of the game. Most come to the same conclusion much later in their careers—in their 30s and 40s. You still have plenty of time to effect change and even speed up the pace if you choose.

You can consider going back to school or pursuing additional training or dedicating more time to your job or even changing directions altogether. It's far more challenging to do this in your 30s or 40s (or later), when you have a family to feed and piles of bills to pay. People do it, but it's harder.

So you're ahead of the game, and you have some options. Now, how about a reality check? Are you really not making progress on your goals or is it all just going a bit slower than you had planned?

If it's the latter, I refer you back to Chapter Three. This whole business of setting and achieving goals takes time. You simply may need to maintain patience and ride out some bumps in the road. If you're already chomping at the bit, feeling as if you're still at the starting gate while the other horses are halfway down the track, you have to ask yourself whether or not you set realistic goals for yourself, and whether it's time to modify them. You also have to ask yourself how long you delayed the real world.

If your goals are realistic, and you really aren't making progress, be honest with yourself: have you put in the work that would yield progress? Would it help to sit down with your supervisor to clarify what it will take to accelerate your development, responsibility, and earnings potential?

Realize that getting ahead likely will require you to abbreviate your social calendar for awhile. You'll probably have to log more hours at the office, take more work home with you, and even volunteer to take on more assignments—especially those that will gain you recognition.

At the end of the day, the only person you can depend on to get ahead is yourself. You'll need to learn to get things done on your own, exhibit excellence, be self-motivated, and drive inspiration from within.

## i FEEL LiKE i'M ALWAYS BEHiND SCHEDULE. ANY TRiCKS FOR MANAGiNG TiME SO i CAN DO SOMETHiNG BESiDES WORK, EAT, AND SLEEP?

Do a quick poll among your friends and co-workers. The topic: what's your morning ritual? Ask them what they do first thing each morning, after settling down at their desks. The responses will probably sound familiar.

When I've asked the question, the most frequent responses tend to fall into one of two categories.

> 1) Check email.
>
> 2) Click onto favorite Internet sites.
>
> 3) Instant message a few friends.
>
> 4) Catch up on the national and international news and my favorite blogs.

You came of age with the Internet, so in some ways, you probably don't appreciate how dramatically technology has transformed our abilities to perform on the job. I still get jazzed that I can use Skype and talk to my friends in Asia for free! But we all also know first-hand what a distraction technology can be. And not only using it, but keeping up with it, not to mention getting it working, takes time as well.

If the first thing you do every morning is click onto the Internet, check your email, and do some instant messaging—or all three—consider what's at stake. One absorbing article on Salon.com and you can blow through ten minutes. A couple notices about new friends at LinkedIn.com and that's another 20. A few IMs about your weekend and you can pretty much kiss an hour or more of your day goodbye.

A recent poll from America Online and Salary.com revealed that employees waste an average of two hours per day. Two hours! If time management is a struggle for you, clearly you're not alone. Most people are not effective time managers, and their productivity is greatly compromised as a result.

An even more recent report by *Advertising Age* Editor-at-Large Bradley Johnson said that 35 million workers—that's one in four workers in the U.S. labor force—spend an average of 3.5 hours, or 9 percent, of each workweek reading blogs. He calls it the "blogification of the workplace" and says it's a major concern. And this is in addition to the time employees already spend surfing the Web.

> I have lots of friends. I chat with over 300 people online who are now my friends. If I want to talk finance, I have a group of advisors online. If I want to talk about movies, there's a chat room with my friends. If I want to find out what's going on in India where I'm from, I have friends online . . . and yeah, sometimes we chat or IM during work, but it's no big deal.

I include this blog business not to encourage you to join the bandwagon, but to ask, if you find your day slipping by and your to-do list getting longer, are you one of these blogified workers?

The key to time management is planning—plain and simple. Fast forward to the end of the day and ask yourself, "What do I need to accomplish before I go to sleep?" Then create a to-do list with those things you identify as your top priorities, and plan your day, including, yes, work things like meetings and appointments, but also personal things like "make dentist appointment," "pick up dry cleaning," "mail sister's birthday gift," and "find outfit for Friday's party."

If you start every day with this sort of planning, you're less likely to let an unexpected email or a flat tire throw you entirely off course, because you'll know what you do and don't have time for. You can reprioritize if necessary. I know to-do lists are not rocket science, but, for many, actually using them is.

The problem for many is they over-list and over-plan. Here's the thing: You can't plan 100 percent of your time. That's just not realistic. You know your boss is going to come in with some last-minute request, or there will be a traffic jam that sets you back an hour. Build in a cushion every day to cover these things—ideally 20 percent of your time.

"Hey, wait a minute!" you say, "20 percent of an eight-hour day is more than an hour and a half—and I typically work more than an eight-hour day! Where am I going to find that kind of time?" Well, how about that two hours per day that most employees waste on personal stuff?

Staying productive from day to day—making the most of your time—requires good organization and not a small degree of discipline. Organization starts with that daily to-do list. Then it means staying conscious of all the potential time killers out there (see below) and forcing yourself to not let them get the best of you.

## POTENTiAL TiME KiLLERS AND THEiR ANTiDOTES

### EMAIL

Check your inbox a few times a day, rather than as soon as emails come in, making sure to respond to all messages within 24 hours and only urgent ones immediately.

### INTERNET

When you need to surf the Internet for business, try to limit distractions by foregoing the compelling story on Your MSN about Paris Hilton's latest fling. And remember, you leave a trail of the sites you visit, so keep it clean and save the Texas Hold 'em for your own personal PC.

### TELEPHONE

Send calls to voice mail when you don't have time.

### CHATTY CO-WORKERS

Tell them you're on deadline and will find time to talk later. "How about lunch?"

### PROCRASTINATION

Dangle instant-gratification carrots in front of yourself to keep motivated. "As soon as I get this done, I'll take myself out for ice cream." Maybe for you it's shoes, the bars, or a nap. Long term the carrots could be a raise, promotion, or your dream job!

I'M NOT GETTING AHEAD, HELP!

Who says you have to answer the phone every time it rings? That's what voice mail is for. If you're on deadline and you have the liberty to do so, screen calls, then plan the time to return them.

If people drop by your desk unexpectedly, kindly let them know you only have a fixed amount of time to talk. If you don't accomplish a task within the time you've allotted for it, my advice is to stay on schedule anyway. Move on to the next thing on your list, and make a note to make time to get back to the unfinished business later.

If you find yourself procrastinating or otherwise avoiding a particularly dreaded task, like standing in line at the post office or going to the dentist, just do it. Better to get that dreaded thing done than spend days avoiding it, right?

Do you have some great time management
techniques you would like to share?
Go to www.NoMoreRamenOnline.com

# WHEN WiLL i SEE RESULTS FROM MY WORK?
It takes a lot more time than you realize to make a difference, whether it's helping others or advancing in your career.

Think about what it takes to rehabilitate a sprained ankle. Immediately after the trauma incident, you keep your foot elevated, apply ice, and pop pain relievers. After the swelling goes down, you begin physical therapy. In early stages, pain actually heightens, and you feel worse, not recognizing any immediate benefits. Eventually, you heal and realize that by taking all these incremental steps you have actually accelerated the rehabilitation and improved your chance of a full recovery.

The same scenario applies in the business world. Immediate results are not always evident. But by staying the course, showing up day after day, and doing a good job on the work you're assigned, you will improve your chance of success.

Patience is part of the program, and you may in fact be making progress, but not know it until you turn around and look.

# WHAT'S THE QUICKEST WAY FOR ME TO ADVANCE ON THE JOB?

One of my co-authors got a job at a marketing communications company right out of college. Her first assignments were little more than making copies, picking up lunch, and buying office supplies. Now two years into the job, she's producing videos, writing newsletters, developing websites, and doing the work she loves.

The same sort of development structure exists in many industries—banking, law, management consulting. Senior-level types invariably delegate the easier stuff to the new recruits. Sometimes the work may seem menial, so it's no surprise when the new recruits say they want to advance as quickly as possible. It's human nature to want what seems like the glamour detail and the healthier paycheck. But the reality is you'll have to do the small stuff well. No one's going to trust you with the big stuff without a solid track record. You have to perform and that means both quality and quantity of results.

Employers want you to grow and develop. Remember, they're investing in your potential. As you become more capable and more productive, you will advance. The question is how long will it take? Along the way, you learn the business. You build a track record of experience and results. You also build your network—inside and outside your company.

That's what you should concentrate on—delivering consistently excellent work, demonstrating business literacy, and expanding your network. Those are the keys to advancement. The faster you ramp them up, the faster you will advance. It's as simple as that.

Clearly, however, this takes a measure of patience. Paying dues doesn't happen overnight, so you have to find it within yourself to stay motivated and focused on the big picture even as you make those daily sandwich runs. Also, don't discount the benefits to be gained from making your boss look good. But it's more than just looking good. One executive told me that he hires people who help make his life easier. Why have people around if they make life harder? Make life easier for others around you, including your boss, and you'll advance.

## i WANT TO BE KNOWN AS AN iMPACT PLAYER—SOMEONE WHO GETS CALLED iNTO THE iMPORTANT MEETiNGS BECAUSE i DELiVER. HOW DO i ACCOMPLiSH THAT?

After a short time on the job, you will likely begin to notice people who take an active role in identifying and complaining about problems, but fail to offer insight or creative ideas about how to resolve the problems. Those people are not impact players. They make life harder, not easier.

When was the last time you rolled up your sleeves and volunteered to take on a challenge facing your organization? Have you ever? Most people sit back and assume the challenge is someone else's responsibility. They wait to be asked to help. But if you take initiative, align the proper resources, and step up to challenges, you eventually make a difference in the outcome. You become an impact player, and no doubt this is how you want to be recognized. Impact players contribute answers and solutions, not just questions and certainly not complaints.

# HOW TO LAND IN THE BOARDROOM

**IF YOU WANT TO MAKE YOUR
WAY INTO THAT BOARDROOM,
THEN FOLLOW THESE GUIDELINES.**

## STOP SAYING THINGS LIKE . . .

I don't see how this plan will work; there's not enough time.

There's no way we have enough money to pull off this project.

We can't possibly find a person who can design this product.

My boss is clueless if she thinks this direction is
going to make any difference at all.

I can't work with so and so.

## START SAYING THINGS LIKE . . .

Time is going to be tight; maybe we can divide the tasks and conquer.

Money may be an issue; let's negotiate with our supplier, explain
our situation, and get them to partner with us on this.

We don't have anyone on staff who can design this product;
let me call a few people I know who may be able to help.

I'm optimistic this direction will make a difference, and
I'm going to give my all so it has the best shot.

Let's assemble the required team, detail individual roles,
and agree on a desired outcome.

# HOW CAN i USE PERFORMANCE REViEWS TO MY ADVANTAGE?

If you work at a large firm, odds are the Human Resources Department has hatched up a structured performance review program. The objective is to ensure that you sit down with your manager on a regular basis to talk about what's going well and what needs to be improved.

At some companies, you'll have formal performance reviews twice a year. Others do it quarterly. One thing you can be sure of is the review will be preceded by paperwork. Most of the time, you'll be asked to review your performance and development objectives and rate how well you've progressed. You'll be asked to outline new development objectives, which is yet another time when knowing your personal goals will prove valuable.

If you do good work—and I'll assume you do—performance review time should really be something to look forward to. Yes, filling out all the paperwork may be time consuming, but think of it this way: You'll be getting paid for 30 minutes or an hour to sit there and have your ego boosted. I don't know anyone who doesn't appreciate hearing from time to time that they're doing a good job. Who knows, there may even be a bonus in there for you!

The performance review is an opportunity to remind your boss how lucky he or she is to have you on the team. To bolster your case, I suggest you keep an accomplishments log. Trust me, your boss won't remember every time you go the extra mile to complete a project or help a client. It's really not her job, so you'll want to make it part of yours. That's what the accomplishments log is for. Keep it up to date and bring a copy to your review meeting. It will only help your cause.

In addition to patting your back, a good manager will use review time to provide feedback about aspects of the job you need to work on. You may be inclined to react to this as critique. It may put you a bit on the defensive, and your first instinct may be to make excuses for yourself. If that's the case, I suggest you do whatever it takes to silence your inner monologue and just listen. Not only is the critique the most valuable aspect of the whole meeting, but your manager probably also finds it uncomfortable to talk about. Don't make it harder.

Here's an example, if she says she'd like to see you be more receptive to other peoples' ideas at project meetings, and you react by defending your expertise in the project area, not only are you confirming that her critique is accurate, but you also may turn her off to providing you more feedback down the road.

If you spend the time formulating excuses, you miss an incredible opportunity to grow and advance your career. Rather than reacting, make the most of the critique by asking for as much detail as possible about how you can improve. Ask for it in writing. Ask for specific examples of what it's going to take to get you to the next level. This will show that you're open to feedback, that you want to improve, and that you're willing to do what it takes to advance. Do you know how few people do this? You want to set yourself apart and get ahead? This will do it.

Then, use the feedback. Make the skills you're working on known to the others you're working with, so they can help find you opportunities to work on them.

If your manager says she'd like to see you provide more ideas at brainstorming meetings, plan to start approaching the meeting organizers in advance, so you can get the information you need to verse yourself and formulate some good ideas ahead of time. Then at the meetings, deliver. If one of your ideas becomes the route the team decides to go with, note it in your accomplishments log for your next performance review.

# HOW OFTEN WiLL i GET A RAiSE? HOW MUCH SHOULD i EXPECT?
The last question addressed performance reviews, so it seems a natural progression that we would move to talking about money. If you're performing well, you should be getting paid accordingly, right? Show me the money! Performance review time also is often when an up tick in pay gets doled out.

Unfortunately, there are no rules for how often you should expect a raise. Sometimes it will follow an annual performance review. Sometimes colleagues will leave the company, opening up a higher-paying spot for you to advance into. Or new projects may arise that will require more time and more responsibilities, for which your employer is willing to compensate you a bit more. There's really no saying.

The question of how much, on the other hand, is a bit more established. Usually it's calculated as a percentage of your current salary. On average, the most you can reasonably expect in a raise is several points higher than the national inflation rate. So if that's what you're looking at, you're doing pretty well.

More often, raises will come in single-digit percentage increments (e.g., 5 percent; 8 percent) unless the raise is accompanied by a promotion. Your raise will likely reflect your performance, and the company's overall performance. You may be kicking butt on the job, but if the company is only puttering along, you really can't expect much. That's when you'll see 2 percent and 3 percent raises —or in the worst of cases, pay cuts if things are really dire.

This is another reason why it's important to negotiate a salary that's acceptable to you when you first take a job. It sets the bar, which doesn't tend to move in leaps and bounds much during your first few years on the job.

## WHAT DO i DO iF i'M OVERLOOKED FOR A PROMOTiON?

This actually happened to me. Here's how I could have responded. I could have made a scene in my boss's office. I could have made life miserable for the person who actually got the position. I could have quit. Instead, I kept working hard, delivering results, and when the person they promoted didn't pan out, and even the one they promoted after him, they turned to me. Patience, maturity, and determination paid off. That's what you do if you're overlooked for a raise.

## HOW DO i MAKE THE MOST OF NETWORKiNG?

Just how socially comfortable are you? Are you cool with going online to Craigslist.com or MySpace.com or trolling around one of a billion interest group sites, everything from chats on cognitive science to the latest government conspiracy theories and back to Cuban hip hop music and its influence on popular culture? Well, yes, that's networking. It's meeting people, and meeting people is critical to your future in terms of work, fun, relationships, even making a difference in the world. Most of my co-authors were pretty at ease in social situations, whether they were online or in person. It was migrating into the more professional world, where, let's face it, older people are that was hard. All of a sudden you're not among a group of people your own age, with similar experiences. You're in this foreign world and you wonder if you'll ever fit in.

Well, it's easy to retreat back to the comfort of your space in MySpace, but eventually you'll want to go beyond. You'll have to go beyond. Why? Because—and I know this is so cliché—it's not what you know, it's who you know. Eventually you'll need to go beyond the space you're in, in person, to get in front of the people who will help you realize your dreams.

It takes a certain amount of nerve to join a chat room that is well underway. It takes a certain amount of nerve to pick up the phone and make that call to an important contact, and it takes a certain amount of nerve to walk into a room full of strangers and feel confident. And everyone is different. The chat room may be a breeze to you, but to another, the room of strangers is an exciting adventure. Others may rock on the phone.

Becoming a solid networker is key to getting ahead in your career and even in your personal life. Yes, dating websites are the rage, but whether you meet someone from a friend or a dating service, you're networking. I don't know many boyfriends or girlfriends who landed on a doorstep without some assistance.

Networking can help you become more productive and efficient, because you deepen your list of contacts about different subjects, industries, companies, etc. They can help you with a work project or help you figure out why your car isn't starting.

Networking puts you in touch with people who can open doors for you—for instance, to a company you've always wanted to work for. One of my co-authors was bold enough to just pick up the phone and call a top executive at the *Houston Chronicle* to see if he knew anyone who was hiring in the news business and got three names and an interview. But some of our other co-authors admitted that they were working at jobs they hated because they were too chicken to make the call at all.

The whole process, whether online, on the phone, or in person, starts with getting comfortable with yourself. Forget about needing to get comfortable in crowds: when you're comfortable with yourself, you're comfortable around others. That's probably why online networking is so pervasive. It allows you to still be out there without being totally at ease with who you are.

I wish there was an easy formula for being okay with yourself. That's a whole week's worth of shows on *Oprah* or better yet, *Dr. Phil*. I am neither of those. So instead, I'm going to give you a few pointers particularly for the face-to-face networking that will get you over your uneasiness and help you fit in with a room full of people from 21 to 81, even if it is heavily slanted to the latter.

First of all, know that older people love talking to younger people. They really do. But be aware that you may have to answer a few lame questions like, "So what are your plans for the future?," to which you'll have three minutes to answer before they start giving you advice. Okay, all that aside, make the best of it because these people actually can help you more than they annoy you. They know people, they can introduce you to people, they can give you a job, they might even have a hottie for a son or daughter. It can happen!

Kidding aside, let's say you are at a Public Relations Society of America cocktail party. It's a great place to meet owners of PR firms, so if you're looking for a job in PR, you should be there. Start out by deciding you are going to meet one, two, three, ten new people, however many you decide. Introducing yourself is as easy as walking up and saying, "Hi, I don't believe we've met." Then ask questions to learn more about them.

There are tons of books about networking. You're probably already a pro online, but if your face-to-face skills need more polish, try *Nonstop Networking: How to Improve Your Life, Luck, and Career*

I'M NOT GETTING AHEAD, HELP!

# QUESTIONS THAT START GREAT CONVERSATIONS

**HERE ARE SOME ICEBREAKERS TO GET PEOPLE TALKING ABOUT THEMSELVES, WHICH THEY LOVE.**

I noticed you're from Philadelphia

Me too.  How long have you lived there?

What brought you to this event today?

How do you know the hosts?

How long have you been part of this organization?

What are some of the best ways to get more involved?

# RULES OF THE FACE-TO-FACE NETWORKING GAME

**BEFORE YOU RUN OUT AND START WALKING UP TO PEOPLE AND ASKING QUESTIONS AT THE NEXT MIXER, REMEMBER THESE RULES OF THE GAME.**

Always approach people who are standing alone.

If no one's standing alone, approach groups of three or more.

Never approach two people who are mid-conversation.

If you drink, don't get drunk even if it does loosen you up.

**HERE ARE A FEW NETWORKING FOLLOW-UP TIPS.**

Obtain a business card from any new contact.

On the back, write detailed information about where you met the person, what he or she does, and what you can do or need from the person.

The next day, transfer the information into your electronic database.

Send a follow-up email: "I really enjoyed meeting you last night and I look forward to. . . ."

or *The Networking Survival Guide: Get the Success You Want by Tapping Into the People You Know.* Nearly all the job sites have networking capabilities now and, of course there's a new breed of referral sites like KarmaOne.com. There are also interest websites, from Aerospace to Xeriscapes and every letter of the alphabet in between. The key is to become a network master regardless of the way you do it. Use the little tricks to make yourself comfortable and pretty soon you will be. Then networking, whether it's online, on the phone, or in person, will just be another hour or two with friends, new and old.

## i'M HAViNG DiNNER WiTH A CLiENT. WHAT SHOULD i KEEP iN MiND?

This shouldn't be funny, but sometimes, real life comes so close to a Ben Stiller movie that you just can't help laughing. I knew a young woman who was invited out for barbeque at one of Texas's best ribs houses. She was new to her job and really wanted to make a good impression. She did everything right. She placed her napkin on her lap, she placed her bread on the right plate, she even ordered a nice healthy portion of barbequed ribs just so everyone knew she could hold her own. She was entertaining and fun. It was a great dinner, that is until she stood up and realized that sometime between the salad with ranch dressing and the last rib, her napkin had fallen off her lap and she had been wiping her barbeque-sauce-laden hands on her skirt. There was no graceful way out of that one. It was a *There's Something About Mary* kind of moment.

Okay, so this kind of thing *can* happen. Bad things like spilling a glass of wine, losing your way from the bathroom, or calling your dinner companion by the wrong name can be overlooked if you are not a complete social oaf the rest of the time.

Some of the rules are fairly obvious. For example, mind your manners. Water glass is on your right. Bread plate on your left. Don't eat until everyone is served. Follow your client's lead on alcohol—yes or no and what variety. Take small bites, and don't talk with food in your mouth.

Now, beyond the things your parents should have taught you, there are the more subtle aspects. For starters, where to go? If the dinner is on your turf, be prepared to offer suggestions that your client will like. Easiest way to figure that out? Dial his assistant and ask what type of food he enjoys or if there is no preference, just say "I personally am a huge Italian food fan, and I always enjoy the opportunity to take people to Little Italy when they're visiting New York." It's better to suggest than to say, "I don't care where we go, wherever you want to go."

Then there's the matter of conversation. Matters of business will inevitably come up—it's at least one thing you have in common, after all. There are two schools of thought about talking business after hours. Some say don't do it. They endorse using the time to get to know each other a bit better and take the relationship to "higher ground." Others say business is why you're there in the first place, and you absolutely should use the time to further endear yourself and your company to the person.

I'm of the latter opinion, but recognize that the business talk may not actually take place until dessert. Think through your agenda of what you want to accomplish, but be flexible as to when it happens. Keep business talk conservative—no hard sales pitches or subjects that will give your dinner companion an ulcer—and keep it brief. Ask open-ended questions, and don't talk excessively about yourself or about people your client doesn't know. There's nothing worse than spending time with someone who just talks and talks and talks and talks and talks and . . . (You get the idea.)

As for the bill, if the person makes a move to pay, graciously decline the offer. If he or she continues to insist, take a second stand, but if it turns into a battle between you and a relentless check stealer, then offer to pay at least your share. If the response is no, offer the tip. If the response remains no, thank them as graciously as you would thank the Queen for tea and say next time it is your treat, then set up the next engagement when you send the thank you note. Understand that if you asked someone out for a meal, it better be one heck of a fight for the check for you to get out of paying.

# iS iT OKAY TO CALL iN "SiCK" TO WORK? Well,

people do. And is it okay? Yeah if you are really sick, contagious, and your company offers sick time. That way you have time to recover, keep germs away from others, and you don't lose any pay. Is it okay when you've partied a little too hard the night before or you just feel like taking advantage of a sick day and you're perfectly fine? No, it isn't okay. It's irresponsible, dishonest, and unethical. Besides that parental barrage, having people cover for you too often and they'll either find a replacement or realize you weren't that important anyway. They are all career killers!

You may argue that it's time your company owes you anyway; after all you get five paid sick days a year. I don't see it that way. If you need a personal day, just ask for it. Most real jobs treat you like an adult and so long as you get the work done, your manager will be reasonable. If, on the other hand, you aren't performing, don't be surprised if the answer is no. Besides, most employees aren't good enough actors to get away with truly faking a sick day. That "sick voice" you practiced and think is so convincing is about as thin as your story. People aren't stupid and faking sickness only makes you look bad.

Look at it this way. When you fake a sick day, you let down your manager and everyone you work with, too. Unlike when you're in school and your profs really couldn't have cared less if you showed up for class, your co-workers do care. Your team cares. Would the New England Patriots care if Tom Brady, their quarterback, blew off the week 12 game because there was great powder on the slopes in Vail? When you let your team down, not only is it unfair to them, but lots of times, they're forced to cover for you. They end up looking like heroes and you end up looking like a weak link. That's just the way the real world is. It's competitive and people around you will look for ways to advance, sometimes at your expense and especially when you make it so darn easy.

## HOW WILL TRENDS IN THE JOB MARKET IMPACT (OR IMPEDE) MY PROGRESS?

As the late-90s dot-com bubble and the ensuing burst demonstrate, the overall market economy has oodles to do with employment prospects. Bull markets can make it the best of times and bear markets the worst. Graduating classes of 1998 faced a profoundly different job market than the one their compadres did a year earlier or three years later.

As history shows, the market will go hot again; it will go down again. It will stay sideways for years. It's cyclical, and next time it spikes, you may very well enjoy some spoils. The problem is no one can predict when the bulls will run.

In lieu of advances in the overall economy, growth in the industry you're in can be the best thing to ever happen to you. Why is that so important? Companies in these sectors often move at a faster pace than those in slow-growth or no-growth industries. Often that means your potential to advance is not only better, but it can happen faster. I mean, if they are growing, they are likely hiring. If they are hiring, they likely need more managers. If they need more managers, you might just get promoted. Contrast that with a company that hasn't increased in size in ten years. You could wait a decade for someone to leave or retire before getting a chance to move up.

If you put aside being in the right industry and the right company, your progress is a factor of the quality of work you submit and your willingness to take on projects. Build a track record of success and an education and skill base that's in high demand, and you won't have to worry about changing market conditions. You'll be better able to adapt with the times, because most assuredly, the times will continue to change.

So getting ahead is as much about personal performance as it is about market performance. It's about posing solutions, not problems, and making your boss's life easier. It's also about recognizing and touting your own accomplishments. Finally it's about networking successfully and getting yourself in front of people who can get you in front of other people who can further your hopes and dreams. To do it right either online, on the phone, or face to face, it means you are comfortable in your own skin and are beginning to really mesh with the adult world. Getting ahead and maturing go hand in hand.

# RESOURCES

## THESE ARE SUGGESTED RESOURCES FROM BOTH 20-SOMETHINGS AND THE AUTHOR.

For a more complete list refer to Additional Resources (see page 228).

www.mindtools.com

www.about.com/careers

www.KarmaOne.com

# 7

# i DON'T KNOW JACK ABOUT MONEY

"I'M LEAVING GRAD SCHOOL OWING more than $120,000 and I'm dreading the day that loan comes due. I think it's going to hit me like a truck. I'm not sure how to handle that kind of debt and get a start in life. I think that's the thing that worries me the most."

# TiME iS ON YOUR SiDE

Lately it seems you can't go a week without seeing or hearing about how deeply in debt Americans are. Take students for example. On average, today's graduates finish their degrees with more accumulated debt than any previous generation. According to a recent survey by the American Council on Education, average debt is often in the tens of thousands of dollars. Sums equal to home mortgage down payments or, in some cases, if you've attended an Ivy League graduate program, the entire mortgage itself. Regardless of what kind of job you'll eventually get, these loans will likely take years to repay.

Of course, this probably isn't news to you. My guess is you're one of those people who recently signed the dotted line on a repayment schedule that stretches past any sort of clear vision you have for your future. That's a scary prospect. Not to mention that student loans are only part of what you will have to deal with monthly. There's also monthly rent, utility bills, cell phone bills, and insurance premiums to manage.

Yes, when it comes to money matters, you must be thinking, "Will I ever be able to afford anything more than ramen?" I'm afraid the answer is not as clear as you'd like it to be. The answer is, "Well, that depends on you."

I hope it helps to know that your salary will probably never be less than what it is on your first job. Unless you choose it to be, that is. You know, you may decide to spend less time on the job and more time with your children or you may decide to quit your job on Wall Street, move to L.A., and try to make it as a rapper. But in all seriousness, you may decide that the six figure salary isn't worth it if what you really want to do is pursue your dream as an artist, teacher, social worker, parent, entrepreneur, or anything else that doesn't pay as well—at least not at the outset. That's a question of sacrifice and priority and we talked about that earlier in this book.

# MY M.O.
# (MONEY OPERANDI)

**THE AMOUNT OF MONEY YOU MAKE IS
ONLY PART OF THE PERSONAL FINANCE EQUATION.
HOW MUCH MONEY YOU HAVE IS ALSO ABOUT WHAT
YOU DO WITH THE MONEY YOU MAKE AND YOUR
ATTITUDE ABOUT MONEY IN GENERAL.
WHAT KIND OF MONEY PERSON ARE YOU?
TAKE THIS LITTLE QUIZ TO FIND OUT.
ARE THESE STATEMENTS TRUE OR FALSE?**

I have no idea how much I am making, really.

I don't know how much money I need to live on.

I'm not sure how much I am spending
in any given month.

I don't really know what I spend my money on.

I've got at least one credit card that
I'm making minimum payments on.

I am saving nothing right now.

If you answered true, to any of these statements, read on,
because this chapter could mean the difference
between financial freedom and financial strife.

# HOW DO PEOPLE ACTUALLY GET AHEAD, I MEAN FiNANCiALLY?

Are you okay with living paycheck to paycheck? Or would you rather be able to drop $300 on a weekend trip without feeling guilty and strapped come the end of the month? It's up to you. The good news is that if you start off right, financial freedom gets easier, not harder and that's really what we're talking about here. The happiness that comes from knowing that financially you are set.

First of all, short of winning the lottery, becoming financially set takes years, even decades in most cases. It's a process that takes time, and here's more good news for people like you in their 20s: Time is your best friend. Before you think, "Great, that means I can keep spending now, I'll have plenty of years down the road to start saving," that's not what I mean. (Nice try, though.) Time is on your side because if you begin saving now, by the time you reach 50 or 60—yes, a long time off—you'll wind up with a lot of money. If you take away nothing else from this book, take away that lesson because if you don't, I guarantee you will be buying lottery tickets when you're 50, praying for a miracle. You don't want to have to work to live in your old age. If you work, you want to do it for the reasons you told me, because you enjoy it. In fact, the surest way to become a working stiff—that person everyone we talked with wants to avoid—is to not save anything while you're young.

The secret to all this time stuff is compound interest. Here's an example:

> Saving $2,000 a year for 40 years is just $80,000. Invest it in an account with annual interest of 10 percent on that money and after 40 years you actually have almost one million dollars. Congratulations, you just won the lottery!

# FREE MONEY!

If you want some real fun, check out this chart that shows how much money you'll have if you put $2,000 away every year, and then escalate the amount you save to $3,000, $4,000 and then to $5,000. If you want to download it, go to the toolbox at www.NoMoreRamenOnline.com.

| YEAR | YOUR ANNUAL CONTRIBUTIONS | CUMULATIVE RETURNS @ 7% | CUMULATIVE RETURNS @ 10% |
|---|---|---|---|
| 1 | $2,000 | $2,070 | $2,100 |
| 2 | $2,000 | $4,285 | $4,410 |
| 3 | $2,000 | $6,655 | $6,951 |
| 4 | $2,000 | $9,191 | $9,746 |
| 5 | $2,000 | $11,904 | $12,821 |
| 6 | $2,000 | $14,807 | $16,203 |
| 7 | $2,000 | $17,914 | $19,923 |
| 8 | $2,000 | $21,238 | $24,015 |
| 9 | $2,000 | $24,794 | $28,517 |
| 10 | $2,000 | $28,600 | $33,469 |
| 11 | $2,000 | $32,672 | $38,915 |
| 12 | $2,000 | $37,029 | $44,907 |
| 13 | $2,000 | $41,691 | $51,498 |
| 14 | $2,000 | $46,680 | $58,747 |
| 15 | $2,000 | $52,017 | $66,722 |

| YEAR | ANNUAL CONTRIBUTIONS | CUMULATIVE RETURNS @ 7% | CUMULATIVE RETURNS @ 10% |
|---|---|---|---|
| 1 | $2,000 | $2,070 | $2,100 |
| 2 | $2,000 | $4,285 | $4,410 |
| 3 | $2,000 | $6,655 | $6,951 |
| 4 | $2,000 | $9,191 | $9,746 |
| 5 | $2,000 | $11,904 | $12,821 |
| 6 | $2,000 | $14,807 | $16,203 |
| 7 | $2,000 | $17,914 | $19,923 |
| 8 | $2,000 | $21,238 | $24,015 |
| 9 | $2,000 | $24,794 | $28,517 |
| 10 | $2,000 | $28,600 | $33,469 |
| 11 | $3,000 | $33,707 | $39,965 |
| 12 | $3,000 | $39,172 | $47,112 |
| 13 | $3,000 | $45,019 | $54,973 |
| 14 | $3,000 | $51,275 | $63,621 |
| 15 | $3,000 | $57,969 | $73,133 |

| YEAR | YOUR ANNUAL CONTRIBUTIONS | CUMULATIVE RETURNS @ 7% | CUMULATIVE RETURNS @ 10% | YEAR | ANNUAL CONTRIBUTIONS | CUMULATIVE RETURNS @ 7% | CUMULATIVE RETURNS @ 10% |
|---|---|---|---|---|---|---|---|
| 16 | $2,000 | $57,728 | $75,494 | 16 | $3,000 | $65,132 | $83,596 |
| 17 | $2,000 | $63,839 | $85,144 | 17 | $3,000 | $72,796 | $95,105 |
| 18 | $2,000 | $70,378 | $95,758 | 18 | $3,000 | $80,997 | $107,766 |
| 19 | $2,000 | $77,374 | $107,434 | 19 | $3,000 | $89,772 | $121,693 |
| 20 | $2,000 | $84,861 | $120,277 | 20 | $3,000 | $99,161 | $137,012 |
| 21 | $2,000 | $92,871 | $134,405 | 21 | $4,000 | $110,242 | $154,913 |
| 22 | $2,000 | $101,442 | $149,946 | 22 | $4,000 | $122,099 | $174,604 |
| 23 | $2,000 | $110,613 | $167,040 | 23 | $4,000 | $134,786 | $196,265 |
| 24 | $2,000 | $120,426 | $185,844 | 24 | $4,000 | $148,361 | $220,091 |
| 25 | $2,000 | $130,926 | $206,529 | 25 | $4,000 | $162,886 | $246,300 |
| 26 | $2,000 | $142,160 | $229,282 | 26 | $4,000 | $178,428 | $275,130 |
| 27 | $2,000 | $154,182 | $254,310 | 27 | $4,000 | $195,058 | $306,843 |
| 28 | $2,000 | $167,044 | $281,841 | 28 | $4,000 | $212,852 | $341,728 |
| 29 | $2,000 | $180,807 | $312,125 | 29 | $4,000 | $231,892 | $380,100 |
| 30 | $2,000 | $195,534 | $345,437 | 30 | $4,000 | $252,264 | $422,310 |
| 31 | $2,000 | $211,291 | $382,081 | 31 | $5,000 | $275,098 | $469,792 |
| 32 | $2,000 | $228,152 | $422,389 | 32 | $5,000 | $299,530 | $522,021 |
| 33 | $2,000 | $246,192 | $466,728 | 33 | $5,000 | $325,672 | $579,473 |
| 34 | $2,000 | $265,496 | $515,501 | 34 | $5,000 | $353,644 | $642,670 |

| YEAR | YOUR ANNUAL CONTRIBUTIONS | CUMULATIVE RETURNS @ 7% | CUMULATIVE RETURNS @ 10% |
|---|---|---|---|
| 35 | $2,000 | $286,150 | $569,151 |
| 36 | $2,000 | $308,251 | $628,166 |
| 37 | $2,000 | $331,898 | $693,083 |
| 38 | $2,000 | $357,201 | $764,491 |
| 39 | $2,000 | $384,275 | $843,040 |
| 40 | $2,000 | $413,245 | $929,444 |
| TOTAL INVESTMENT | $80,000 | | |

| YEAR | ANNUAL CONTRIBUTIONS | CUMULATIVE RETURNS @ 7% | CUMULATIVE RETURNS @ 10% |
|---|---|---|---|
| 35 | $5,000 | $383,574 | $712,187 |
| 36 | $5,000 | $415,599 | $788,656 |
| 37 | $5,000 | $449,866 | $872,771 |
| 38 | $5,000 | $486,531 | $965,298 |
| 39 | $5,000 | $525,764 | $1,067,078 |
| 40 | $5,000 | $567,742 | $1,179,036 |
| TOTAL INVESTMENT | $140,000 | | |

So you may be saying, "I can't save $2,000 per year. I'm only making 26 grand!" Well, I'm not letting you off the hook that easily. Let's break this down first and you be the judge of whether or not it is worth it to save. Two thousand dollars per year is about $167 per month. That's about $42 every week. Divided by 7 days in a week, that's just 6 bucks. Or put in more realistic terms, a vente latte at Starbucks and a Whopper. So here's how you make sure you save $2,000 a year: make your own coffee and your own lunch. Hard to believe it can be that easy, isn't it?

## REBEL AGAiNST THE SYSTEM!

**Pay off your credit card
every month and carry no balance.
The credit card companies will hate you!**

Unfortunately, most Americans somehow can't seem to save anything. They make the mistake of elevating their spending habits to just above their income level, and they panic every time the phone rings, worried that it's a collector asking for payment. They have credit cards loaded with debt and pay just the minimums, ensuring they will never get ahead. That's how the credit card companies want it. They don't make any money off of people who pay their entire bill every month! The best credit card customer is the one who diligently pays the minimums, month after month, and keeps adding to the balance, month after month.

As you might already be understanding, having money is more about good habits than it is about having a huge salary. I have

# PAY OFF YOUR CREDIT CARDS NOW!

IF YOU CARRY A BALANCE OF $3,000 FOR A YEAR,
SEE BELOW TO LEARN HOW MUCH IT REALLY COSTS YOU.
(ANNUAL INTEREST RATE OF 18 PERCENT
OR 1.5 PERCENT PER MONTH.)

| MONTH | AMOUNT OWED | INTEREST ADDED ON | TOTAL PRINCIPAL AND INTEREST | MINIMUM PAYMENTS MADE |
|---|---|---|---|---|
| January | $3000.00 | $45.00 | $3045 | $60.00 |
| February | $2985.00 | $44.78 | $3029.78 | $60.59 |
| March | $2985.00 | $44.54 | $3013.73 | $60.27 |
| April | $2953.46 | $44.30 | $2997.76 | $59.96 |
| May | $2937.80 | $44.07 | $2997.76 | $59.64 |
| June | $2922.23 | $43.83 | $2966.06 | $59.32 |
| July | $2906.74 | $43.60 | $2950.34 | $59.00 |
| August | $2891.34 | $43.37 | $2934.71 | $58.39 |
| September | $2876.02 | $43.14 | $2919.16 | $58.39 |
| October | $2860.78 | $43.14 | $2903.69 | $58.07 |
| November | $2830.53 | $42.68 | $2872.99 | $57.77 |
| December | $2830.53 | $42.46 | $2872.99 | $57.46 |
| Year end balance | $2815.53 | | | |
| Principal reduced by | $184.47 | | Amount you paid | $709.16 |

If you would like to download this chart so you can put it on the fridge or in your car (whatever works to remind you), go to the toolbox at www.NoMoreRamenOnline.com

friends who have never quite gotten this. They make lots of money. They spend everything, When they get laid off or get sick or get into a wreck, they are scrambling. I have even known people whose out-of-control financial situation led them to commit crimes.

So get your financial footing early, and you'll pave the way into your 30s and beyond.

## START BY CREATING A BUDGET One aspect of your working life that you will come to know well is the annual budgeting process. Whether you work for a nonprofit organization or a Fortune 500 company or are managing a construction project, budgeting is key. Companies usually budget in the fall for what they'll spend the next year. Managers piece together lists of expenses—stuff they know of right now like salaries, equipment—and even unexpected costs.

### TIPS FOR MANAGING YOUR BUDGET

Use Quicken or online banking to track your expenses, balance your account, and generate reports.

Use a debit card rather than a credit card so you don't overspend; you can't spend what you don't have with a debit card.

Look at your finances weekly, just to make sure you are on track.

This process is really no different from how you set up your own budget. In a business budget, like your own budget, managers will often want to spend more than they have, but the top executives usually put the kibosh on that. When doing your own budget, you have to be both manager and executive. You have to put the kibosh on your own tendencies to over-spend. So are you ready for your first executive position in the corporation of YOU? Here's your executive training on how to create and manage a budget. For those of you who made it through advanced calculus, bear with how easy this really is.

See, it's not the actual math that's difficult, but rather accepting the fact that the math doesn't lie. It's in coming to terms with the fact that you just can't afford an apartment in Manhattan or a $150 pair of shoes or even a vente latte every day.

The best scenario, of course, is when your income covers your expenses and then some. That's when you have more options. That's when the occasional $150 pair of shoes becomes less burdensome. But it doesn't mean you should be any less scrupulous in how you manage your money. I suggest you keep track of how much you spend in any given category to ensure you use your money the way you want to be using it.

In addition to your long-term savings (remember the $2,000 a year we talked about earlier?), I suggest you take 2 to 3 percent of your gross salary every month and put it into a rainy day fund for things that arise unexpectedly or that you didn't include as part of your budget from the outset (e.g., medical bills, car repair, travel). You can do this by putting your change in a jar, earmarking part of those cash gifts from Mom or Dad, or saving the cash you find in your jean pockets or the dryer. When you get $50 or $100, deposit it.

# THINKING MONTHLY...

## 1. Start by tallying all your fixed monthly expenses:

Rent _____

Groceries _____

Electricity _____

Gas/Oil _____

Water _____

Sewer _____

Phone/Cell Phone _____

Cable/Internet _____

Student loan payments _____

Credit card payments _____
(to pay them off, not minimums)

Car payment _____

Car insurance _____

Car maintenance _____

Commuting (gas, tolls, train, etc.). _____

Health insurance _____

**2. Next, tally the sum of all your discretionary expenses:**

Gym membership _____

Eating out _____

Entertainment (bars, movies, vacations, etc.)_____

Clothes _____

Dry cleaning_____

Furniture/décor _____

Subscriptions _____ _____

Giving _____

**3. Next, write down the amount you will save:**

Long-term savings _____

Rainy day fund _____
(car repairs, medical, loss of job, etc.)

**4. Add it all together and you have a snapshot of the amount of money you need to live a certain lifestyle.**

**5. Now compare it to the amount of money you take home every month. If you're like most people, that number adds up to more than you actually make. So avoid the trap of juggling expenses and spending more than you make. Proceed to step 6!**

**6. Adjust your budget by setting targets for each line item. Add up your targets and adjust them until they total your monthly income.**

If you would like to download this template,
go to the toolbox at www.NoMoreRamenOnline.com

# A BiT MORE HELP WiTH BUDGETiNG

**WHAT IF YOU HAVE TO CUT BACK ON YOUR BUDGET?
(AND YOU PROBABLY WILL) HERE'S A SAMPLE
BUDGET YOU CAN USE TO FIGURE OUT WAYS
TO LOWER YOUR EXPENSES IF YOU HAVE TO.**

| MONTHLY BUDGET ITEM | LOW | HIGH | MY PLAN FOR LOWERING | MY MONTHLY TARGET |
|---|---|---|---|---|
| **ESSENTIAL EXPENSES** | | | | |
| RENT | $450 | $1000 | GET A ROOMMATE | $450 |
| GROCERIES | $150 | $300 | EAT AT HOME AND COOK IN VOLUME; TAKE LEFTOVERS TO WORK | $190 |
| ELECTRICITY | $50 | $75 | MONITOR YOUR AIR CONDITIONING OR HEAT, GET A ROOMMATE | $50 |
| GAS/OIL | $100 | $150 | MONITOR YOUR THERMOSTAT TO SAVE ENERGY | $100 |
| WATER | $25 | $50 | CONSERVE WATER, GET A ROOMMATE | $25 |
| SEWER | $20 | $20 | GET A ROOMMATE | $20 |
| CELL PHONE | $60 | $100 | MONITOR MINUTES AND IM'S, GET CELL PHONE THROUGH WORK, USE VOICE-OVER IP | $60 |
| CABLE/INTERNET | $40 | $80 | GET A ROOMMATE, GET RID OF PREMIUM CHANNELS | $60 |
| STUDENT LOAN PAYMENTS | $150 | $750 | SPEAK TO YOUR PARENTS ABOUT HELPING | $150 |
| CREDIT CARD PAYMENTS | $100 | $500+ | PAY OFF IN ONE YEAR | $150 |
| CAR PAYMENT | $220 | $400 | BUY A USED CAR | $220 |
| CAR INSURANCE | $150 | $250 | NO TRAFFIC TICKETS | $187 |
| REGULAR CAR MAINTENANCE/FUEL | $120 | $250 | CARPOOL, DRIVE LESS | $150 |
| HEALTH INSURANCE | $65 | $150 | STAY HEALTHY | $80 |
| COMMUTING | $50 | $120 | CAR POOL, AVOID PEAK TRAFFIC, BUY FUEL-EFFICIENT | $60 |

| MONTHLY BUDGET ITEM | LOW | HIGH | MY PLAN FOR LOWERING | MY MONTHLY TARGET |
|---|---|---|---|---|
| **DISCRETIONARY EXPENSES** | | | | |
| GYM, SPORTS, LEAGUES | $75 | $200 | FIND LOWER RATES | $75 |
| EATING OUT | $75 | $150 | PREPARE MORE MEALS AT HOME | $75 |
| ENTERTAINMENT | $75 | $500 | DON'T GO OUT AS OFTEN OR SPEND LESS WHEN YOU DO | $300 |
| CLOTHES/DRY CLEANING | $100 | $300 | CURB SPENDING, AVOID BUYING DRY-CLEAN-ONLY GARMENTS | $150 |
| FURNITURE/DÉCOR | $150 | $300 | AVOID TEMPTATION TO BUY | $150 |
| SUBSCRIPTIONS | $25 | $80 | READ WORK COPIES | $25 |
| GIVING | $25 | $100 | SAVE MONEY ELSEWHERE TO MAINTAIN LEVEL OF GIVING, GIVE TIME NOT CASH | $50 |
| MISCELLANEOUS | $50 | $120 | WATCH SPENDING ON LITTLE THINGS LIKE SALONS, MAILING, ETC., TAKE ADVANTAGE OF LEGITIMATE PERKS AT WORK, LIKE COFFEE, SNACKS, ETC. | $65 |
| **SAVINGS** | | | | |
| LONG TERM | $1000 PER YEAR | $3000 PER YEAR | JOIN 401(K) PLAN AT WORK, CONTRIBUTE EVERY PAY CHECK | $200 |
| RAINY DAY FUND | $1000 PER YEAR | $3000 PER YEAR | OPEN SAVINGS ACCOUNT | $200 |
| TOTALS | | | | |

If you would like to download this budget template,
go to the toolbox at www.NoMoreRamenOnline.com

# HOW MUCH SHOULD i TRY TO SAVE EVERY MONTH? One of my co-authors joked that he was
just finishing school and he already felt pressure to prepare for
retirement. I bet you can relate to the feeling.

If you've been following the news, you are aware that the future
of our social security system is looking pretty bleak. On top of
that, the other form of societal safety net that our parents and
our parents' parents enjoyed, company pension plans, are few
and far between, too. These days, the only program you can
count on for saving for your retirement is the one you create.

So how will you live comfortably when you are ready to retire,
30- or 40-plus years from the day you started working? The
answer is you need to start saving immediately, even if the
amount is minimal. Start now and you will be in a much better
position later on. Have I said that often enough in this chapter
to make you understand that it's really important?

How much should you be saving? Aim to budget at least 10 percent
of your net income for long-term savings. (This is income after
Uncle Sam has taken his share, which may be 28 percent
or more, plus state taxes and social security.)

## BREAK IT DOWN AS FOLLOWS

- Put 6 percent of your salary, up to the maximum permissible,
  into a company-funded 401(k), IRA, or other retirement plan.
  Do this especially when your employer matches a portion of
  contributions.

- Put the remaining 4 percent aside as a down payment for a house
  or to open up a brokerage account for additional investing.

NO MORE RAMEN

- Put another 2–3 percent aside each month in an emergency fund.

As your income increases, increase the percentage you put into long-term savings. Ideally, make it a majority (70 percent to 80 percent) of the additional money you make each month. Your lifestyle doesn't have to escalate in direct proportion to your increasing pay. In fact, treat yourself to a few extra rewards, but put most of it away.

As important as it is to put the money away, making steady contributions and leaving the money alone is equally important. That's where compound interest makes mountains out of mole hills.

## WHAT iF i HAVE CREDiT CARD DEBT?

If you have credit card debt, you absolutely want to pay that off—fast. Here's why: Most likely the credit card company is charging you more than 15 percent annual interest on the balance you owe. That means for every $100 you owe, they are charging you 1.25 to 1.50 percent per month to carry that balance every month. Over the course of one year that's $15 that you will have to pay above and beyond the $100 you owe. That may not seem like a ton of money, but trust me, it's a license to steal. Check out the chart on page 167 and you'll see why.

In addition, stop using your credit cards; use debit cards instead, since with them you can only spend what you have in the bank. I know it might be hard, but scrimp on everything; eat ramen again until you pay off the cards. Then only charge what you can pay off monthly and make that a plan for life. Sign a pact with yourself that you will never, ever again pay a dime of interest to a credit card company. Accomplish that and you'll be ahead of three-quarters of the population. You can do it.

# HOW DO i BOOST MY CREDiT SCORE?

For as dangerous as credit cards and credit in general can be if not used properly, they are an important tool in life. You will have to buy things on credit, such as a home and sometimes a car. Companies look favorably and offer lower interest rates to people who have better credit scores. And once you sign up for a credit card or buy anything with credit, you have a credit score.

There are lots of sites online where you can find out your current credit score. The most reliable one is www.annualcreditreport.com. This is the site recommended by the Federal Trade Commission and it links you to the three main credit reporting companies: TransUnion, Equifax, and Experian. And you are entitled to one free credit report from each of them per year. Exercise your rights by getting copies and attending to anything that doesn't look right. That way, next time someone asks to run your credit, you'll know exactly what they will discover.

When it comes to credit, failing to make monthly payments, being sent to collections for outstanding debt, or declaring bankruptcy are credit score killers. And just as it's easier to put on five pounds than it is to lose it, it's a lot easier to destroy credit than to rebuild it.

Time figures big into the credit score equation. Continue to be a good debtor for a few years and your score will increase. If you fall in the hole a little bit, focus on repaying existing debts before taking on new ones. Also limit the number of credit accounts you open. Having too many open lines out there—especially ones that you draw on—may make creditors wary of your ability to repay and reduce your score. In general boosting your credit score is about paying your bills on time, being responsible for your debts, and living that philosophy over time.

# WiTH SO MANY OPTiONS OUT THERE, LiKE STOCKS, MUTUAL FUNDS, CDs, BONDS, WHAT SHOULD i START iNVESTiNG iN?

As previously mentioned, I suggest you earmark 10 percent of your net income for long-term investing. The majority should be aimed squarely at a company-funded 401(k) program (or a 403 (b) program if you work for a school, hospital, or nonprofit organization), particularly those for which the employer matches contributions.

The reasons to do this are compelling. First, whether the employer matches 100 percent of your contribution or only 3 percent, to you it's free money. It's cash that's going into an account that bears your name, cash that you will have the pleasure of tapping into later in your life. No strings attached!

Second, 401(k) and 403(b) accounts reduce your current tax bill. If you are earning a $30,000 salary and contribute $2,000 to a tax-deferred savings plan, you pay no taxes on that $2,000 in the current year. In other words, it's like you are only paying taxes on $28,000 of income. You only pay taxes when you retire and begin withdrawing the money.

Third, 401(k) and 403(b) accounts accumulate interest tax deferred. That means you can park your money in an account and invest it as conservatively or aggressively as you wish. Either way, you won't pay a dime of taxes on the interest income it generates for many years to come.

You *can* make an early withdrawal from a tax-deferred savings account. WARNING: Doing so will cost you a significant portion of what you earned. There are significant penalties for early withdrawal.

I DON'T KNOW JACK ABOUT MONEY

Starting out with an employer sponsored 401(k) or 403(b) program also makes sense because it allows you to test the investment waters a bit. Remember, the accounts act a lot like other investment accounts. You decide how you want the money to be invested. However, more often than not, the company programs offer a fixed number of investment vehicles (e.g., mutual funds, bonds, money market funds) for you to choose from so that you can diversify and minimize your exposure should any one of the programs go down in value. This takes a lot of the time and stress out of the research side of things, which you'll want to do to make sure the investments you choose are designed to do what you want them to.

I suggest investing in three different programs, with none of them taking up more than 50 percent of the total. For instance, contribute 40 percent to your favorite (preferably a growth account), 30 percent in a less aggressive program, and 30 percent in a more aggressive program. Depending upon the advice that you get, from family, a financial advisor, or a finance executive at your new employer, you can modify the contributions. Early in your career, it's best to avoid "fixed income" accounts, which are the most conservative but better suited to older people who are protecting their wealth rather than growing it.

It's also good practice for opening up a separate brokerage account for additional investing a few years down the road.

> I'm getting to the point where I want to buy a house.
> But I'm not settled enough in my career. I mean, I'm still
> thinking I may need more education to do what I want to do.
> But I'm concerned because houses are so expensive that if I wait
> any longer I may have to settle for less or settle for an area
> that I don't really want to live in.

Of course, before you invest in anything know what you want to achieve with your investments (goal setting again!). I also think it makes sense to talk with a tax advisor or a financial planner you trust, usually someone referred by a trusted family member or friend, and over time, find reliable working contacts that can confidently refer you to new brokers. When changing directions, do so in safe increments and not all at once, to mitigate risk. Test the new broker out for a period with a smaller percentage of savings (e.g. 20 percent), and if they perform adequately, you can increase your contributions or phase out progressively from the old account.

## MY FRiEND HAS ASKED TO BORROW MONEY. SHOULD i LEND iT TO HiM?

The hard truth is you almost always become the bad guy when you lend money. It's one thing to float a friend $5 or $10 for lunch. If that person forgets to repay you, or you forget to ask, that's not going to be a huge setback. It's another thing entirely if the "forgotten wallet" becomes a pattern.

Remember, there's absolutely no shame in saying you don't have the cash to loan out money. Tell friends who constantly ask that you're on a ramen diet yourself right now, or that you just don't loan money. You could offer your friend help in creating a budget, but unless he or she asks, this could be awkward.

If you do loan out money—whatever the reason—accept that you're not going to see payment any time soon, if ever. Most unsecured credit, which is what a friendly loan is since few people will ask for some item of collateral for the loan, will not be repaid. Worse still, when you loan money to people who can't repay, you may find them avoiding you or treating you differently.

The price of a friendship can be surprisingly small. Yes, I have loaned money to friends in the past and I have gotten burned on more than one occasion. Now I make a habit of not doing it. Unfortunately, I learned my lessons the hard way and not only lost the money but lost a friendship or two.

# WHEN SHOULD i CONSiDER BUYiNG A HOME VS. RENTiNG A PLACE TO LiVE?

One of the more tangible milestones of adulthood is the purchase of your first home. Whether it's a condo, a townhouse, or a property with land, buy property and you stake your flag in the ground. You become part of the community, part of the establishment—or so the logic goes.

## MORTGAGE JARGON

### FIXED-RATE LOANS

Allow you to lock in one interest rate
for the life of the loan.

### ADJUSTABLE-RATE LOANS

The interest rate of the loan can go up or down
based on the prevailing interest rate climate.

### BEST ADVICE

Research at eloan.com, lendingtree.com
and talk to experienced homeowners and the people who
work at your bank to learn the ins and outs about
home loans before you sign on the dotted line.

Let's completely kick to the curb the idea that buying property means you're settling down, because it doesn't. If you wanted to, you could buy a home and put it right back on the market the day you take possession. People who invest in real estate do that every day. But if you have an apartment lease, you may think you have more freedom should you want to move, but the reality is you may not. If you are fortunate to be in a seller's market with really low home interest rates (at the writing of this book, 6 to 7 percent for those with good credit records), you can possibly sell your home for a profit before you can get out of a standard six-month or one-year lease. And there's always the option of becoming a landlord.

I did that when I bought my first house. I lived in it for a year, and then moved out of state to take another job. Rather than sell it (and lose money; the market was down), I rented it. Renters paid most of the mortgage for me, and I now have an income-generating property still appreciating in value. After a few tenuous years during which I learned the landlord game (and hired a good property manager), I diversified my overall investment portfolio and gained experience in the real estate world to invest further when markets were favorable.

When should you buy instead of rent? Obviously, the first question is, do you have cash for a down payment? A $200,000 house may require 10 to 20 percent down to obtain a favorable interest rate.

Next, can you afford the monthly expenses? Sure, monthly mortgage payments often parallel monthly rent fees. (This is no coincidence.) But there are many other fees associated with homeownership to consider. Things like property taxes, association fees, maintenance, and repairs. If you rent, your landlord pays these. If covering these expenses is not feasible, keep renting.

# THE HiGH COST OF RENT

YOUR APARTMENT MAY BE COSTING YOU MORE THAN YOU THINK. AFTER JUST FIVE YEARS IN A HOME, YOU COULD HAVE $30,000 TO $60,000 OR EVEN $90,000 IN EQUITY. WHEN YOU RENT, YOU ARE GIVING THAT MONEY AWAY. WHEN YOU OWN, YOU'RE ESSENTIALLY PUTTING MONEY INTO A BANK THAT YOU CAN LIVE IN, TOO. THAT'S PRETTY SWEET. SEE FOR YOURSELF.

## RENT vs BUY

The table below will help you see how much
you'll spend in rent over the next 1, 5, 10 and 15 years

| IF YOUR CURRENT RENT IS: | 1 YEAR | 5 YEARS | 10 YEARS | 15 YEARS |
|---|---|---|---|---|
| $500 | $6,000 | $30,000 | $60,000 | $90,000 |
| $600 | $7,200 | $36,000 | $72,000 | $108,000 |
| $700 | $8,400 | $42,000 | $84,000 | $126,000 |
| $800 | $9,600 | $48,000 | $96,000 | $144,000 |
| $900 | $9,600 | $54,000 | $108,000 | $162,000 |
| $1,000 | $12,000 | $60,000 | $120,000 | $180,000 |
| $1,100 | $13,200 | $66,000 | $132,000 | $198,000 |
| $1,200 | $14,400 | $72,000 | $144,000 | $216,000 |
| $1,300 | $15,600 | $78,000 | $156,000 | $234,000 |
| $1,400 | $15,600 | $84,000 | $168,000 | $252,000 |
| $1,500 | $18,000 | $90,000 | $180,000 | $270,000 |

From www.homesightwa.org

Then there are questions about your local real estate market that you need to answer. Determine if the market is a seller's market, meaning houses are selling quickly, or if it is a buyer's market, meaning houses are taking time to sell. In a seller's market, you can buy a house, usually at top dollar. If the market keeps going up it could appreciate quickly. Of course, the market could fall and then you may lose a little. If it is a buyer's market, you may be able to find some under-valued property and make money through appreciation when the market rebounds. But that could take years. Before you look at buying a home, know what kind of market cycle your town is in.

## ASK THESE QUESTIONS

- Are more properties for sale than there are buyers to buy them (buyer's market), or is it the opposite (seller's market)?

- How many licenses have been issued to build new homes?

- Is the population growing, staying steady, or declining in your town?

- Can you afford the type of property that you want and that would have resale value? If yes, it's likely a buyer's market.

- How quickly do properties turn over when they're put up for sale? If it is fast, it's a seller's market.

- If you have to move, could you rent it for an amount close to your monthly expenses, or can you handle the additional cash drain while living elsewhere?

When you do envision staying put for the time being (a year or more) and your answers to all the relevant questions are favorable, that's when buying a home begins to make sense.

# WHAT iF i "FORGET" TO FiLE MY TAXES? AND WHEN DOES iT MAKE SENSE TO HiRE AN ACCOUNTANT?

As the saying goes, the only two certainties in life are death and taxes.

Like it or not, once you are part of the work force, the United States Government expects to hear from you on or before April 15 of the following year. "But I didn't make much money!" you say. To find out if you need to file a tax return, go to www.irs.org and click on the Individuals tab. You'll answer some questions and the IRS will tell you if you need to file a return.

Sometimes you'll love the result of your tax return—particularly when you discover you paid the IRS more in taxes than you had to. That nice refund check that arrives in your mailbox from the

Treasury Department is found money! Of course, the opposite can also be true. Whatever you do, don't "forget" to file a return. Not only can doing so make you liable for late fees in addition to tax dollars owed, but it also can damage your credit. Are you getting the message? Don't mess with the IRS!

To help you remember to file, most post offices begin stacking piles of tax booklets and forms around February of every year. Plus it's all over the news come late March and early April. Read the forms to get a sense for which ones apply to your personal financial situation. If you can get away with the EZ forms, filing shouldn't be too much of a burden.

The IRS's "e-file" tool (www.irs.gov) has also made it easier than ever to complete the much-loathed task of filing tax returns. Numerous computer programs (e.g., TurboTax) are also out there. They'll cost you, but they tend to prove handy in finding deductions you wouldn't be aware of otherwise.

Now, if you're just plain miserable at math, or you tend to be-come confused any time the government issues instructions, that's when you should consider hiring help. Also, if your tax return is going to be complicated—for instance, you moved to a new state or you have several sources of income or you worked for more than one employer in the same tax year—then working with a professional might be a good idea.

> One of the great blessings about living
> in a democracy is that we have complete
> control over how we pay our taxes . . .
> cash, check, or money order.
> (Source Unknown)

In these cases, ask a friend, family member, or trusted co-worker, preferably someone who has screened accountants, for a reference or do an Internet search for certified public accountants and/or certified financial planners in your area. You can also go to places like H&R Block, which is in the business of tax preparation. A good accountant or advisor is well worth the fees you pay.

Prepare your taxes in February before the rush. Use January to get all your information together and your receipts if you will be itemizing your return. If you find that you are getting a refund, file your return immediately. The sooner they get your return, the sooner you get your check. If you find that you owe the IRS, then file in April and use the time you have to save the money you need to pay your tax bill. And one more important point: Keep your tax returns—both current and past years!

# i HAD TO LiST HOW MANY DEDUCTiONS i WANTED TO DECLARE WHEN i FiLLED OUT THE TAX FORMS AT MY JOB. WHAT ARE DEDUCTiONS?

Deductions are the number of dependents or people who you're supporting with your salary. Technically when you are single, you should declare one dependent—yourself. But sometimes people choose to declare more than one dependent. Why? Because the more dependents you declare the less taxes your employer deducts from your paycheck. Now before you head over to the Human Resources Department and claim ten dependents, understand that if you don't have the government withhold taxes now, you'll have to pony up the money at the end of the year when you file your tax return. Declare just one deduction because the moral of the story is that you always pay; either now, before you see the money, or later when you have to come up with the money!

# WHAT'S THE DEAL WiTH LiFE iNSURANCE?

I'm guessing that life insurance ranks up there with Jell-O on the list of things you spend time thinking about from day to day. It's not required, like auto insurance. You probably don't have any dependents, meaning kids, to support after you die. You're generally healthy, and you don't plan to die any time soon. So why bother?

Well, first of all, some employers offer life insurance as a benefit. If they offer it, take it. Why not? But if they don't offer it, I submit one reason why you may want to look into it and at least understand it: this is one time your age works in your favor, meaning life insurance is cheaper when you're younger.

Now, it's highly likely that you really have no need for life insurance, but your needs may increase as you age and take on more responsibility. A person buys life insurance to make sure those they love are cared for after he or she dies. Think of it this way: One day you may have a spouse and children, and you may live in a house and have a mortgage payment. If you die, your life insurance will help pay to support your spouse, children, and maybe even pay for the house. The insurance could help pay off debt and even put some coin in the piggy bank so your spouse and kids can sustain the lifestyle they have come to enjoy. It can even pay final expenses. That's what life insurance is at its most basic.

# iS THERE ANY DOWNSiDE TO COLLECTiNG UNEMPLOYMENT BENEFiTS?

The only downside I can see to collecting unemployment is the main factor of eligibility—you have to be out of work to collect.

Actually going to the Department of Economic Security and standing in line can be demoralizing. But how wonderful it is to live in the 21st Century when you can buffer your bruised ego by applying for unemployment benefits by phone or online. But pride aside, you do qualify for checks from the government when your full-time employment ends for reasons out of your control. Don't get too excited, though. The checks are for just a fraction of what you were making, and you can only collect them for so long.

Remember, you can't quit a job and collect unemployment. Technically, you also have to be seeking a new job in order to qualify. Of course, people try to take advantage of the system every day. There's a great *Seinfeld* episode where George tries to scam that he's looking for employment and has an interview at Vandelay industries to be a latex salesman. I believe he ends up flat on his face with his pants down around his ankles. Not a pretty sight.

Bottom line: If you qualify for unemployment, take it. The money will help you make ends meet in between jobs.

Being a good money manager is one of the most critical aspects of succeeding in life. There are no commercials on the TV, radio, or Internet that try to get you to save your money. But there are plenty that help you find ways to spend it. I'm not saying you need to deprive yourself of everything, but I am saying that no one can have everything immediately. If you want to make sure you're not still eating ramen when you're 30, or worse yet, eating ramen on credit, don't overspend. And in a nutshell that means, buy only what you have the cash to pay for today, and put money away for tomorrow.

# RESOURCES

## THESE ARE SUGGESTED RESOURCES FROM BOTH 20-SOMETHINGS AND THE AUTHOR.

For a more complete list refer to Additional Resources
(see page 228).

**www.moneypants.com**

**www.suzeorman.com**

**www.about.com/money**

**www.hrblock.com**

**www.irs.gov**

# 8

# i HAVE TO GET A GRiP ON
# THE DAY TO DAY

"IN COLLEGE I GOT GOOD AT STUDYING, going to class, taking tests, meeting people at parties, but now it's all changed. I'm not meeting as many people, I feel like a fish out of water at my job, I don't know the first thing about stuff like health insurance, and I'm not really dealing with my day to day very well. It's a stressor and I don't know if I'll ever feel like I fit in and know what I'm doing."

# ALL THAT OTHER STUFF. So by now, we've covered the transition from school to work (and back maybe), getting ahead on the job and tending to your financial well being.

I could talk for days about these subjects, but as I've said before, balance is the key to thriving in life. Fact is, between commuting to and from work and squeezing as much fun as possible into the weekends, there are all sorts of things out there to throw you out of balance and weigh you down.

Many of the questions on the minds of my co-authors fell into the "other" category. I imagine you can relate. That's what this chapter is about—all that other stuff that makes your life your life.

## WiLL i EVER GET USED TO THiS 8AM TO 5PM SCHEDULE? RiGHT NOW iT'S KiLLiNG ME. Some things about the workplace continue to evolve. Dress code, for example. Suits and ties were once *de rigueur,* but offices now allow employees to come as you are—to a point, that is. Telecommuting is now a viable option for many people.

In the meantime, other aspects of work have stayed the same, primary among them business hours. If anything, they've gotten longer. And there's really not much you can do about the regimentation other than find work you enjoy doing with people you enjoy being with from eight to five.

Yes, that six am alarm comes as a terribly rude awakening in your first days on the job. But like starting a new exercise routine, it eventually will become tolerable. Scheduling activities for yourself after hours also will prevent you from frittering away entire evenings in front of the TV.

The main thing to keep in mind here is your overall goals. Keep an eye on meeting the incremental objectives and chalk up the workday schedule as a short-term sacrifice for your long-term success. The further along you get in your career, you'll also come to enjoy more flexibility in your schedule.

## i'M ONLY 25 AND i'M AWAKE AT NiGHT WORRYiNG ABOUT THE THiNGS ON MY TO-DO LiST i DiDN'T GET TO. AM i BECOMiNG STRESSED OUT LiKE MY PARENTS? WHAT CAN i DO?

The American Institute of Stress (yes, there is such a place) refers to stress as America's number one health problem. They say, "The stress response of the body is somewhat like an airplane readying for take-off. Virtually all systems—the heart and blood vessels, the immune system, the lungs, the digestive system, the sensory organs, and the brain—are modified to meet the perceived danger." And it sure doesn't take much time in an airport, on a rush-hour commute, or in a shopping mall in December to realize just how widespread stress is in our lives.

Stress causes headaches, nausea, depression, insomnia, and myriad other physical ailments including heart disease and high blood pressure. It makes us do stupid things like flip off that creep who honked at you, regrettable things like yelling at loved ones, and downright ridiculous things like buying diet pills from AsSeenonTV.com.

Stress is a serious issue, I don't deny. But I also have to say, "Accept it right now, because you won't be able to eliminate it from your life." However, you can minimize the bad stress, use the good stress to your advantage, and get better at turning the bad stress into the good. That starts with identifying what stresses you out—it can be different from one person to the next—and learning how to deal with it. It also starts with knowing the difference between good stress (the stuff that gets you energized) and bad stress (the stuff that gets you sick).

It's true, stress isn't always a negative. It can be a real motivator that gets your adrenaline flowing and keeps you plowing forward to accomplish things you didn't think you could ever do. If you're into sports, you know what I'm talking about because it's common for football players or basketball players, for instance, to find the moments leading up to the game stressful. But it's a stress that gets them going; it's a stress they thrive on and a stress that many find hard to live without when they retire into a normal life. Actors and musicians often say the same thing before going on stage.

The stressors that are tough to deal with are the ones that are out of our control—traffic jams that make us late, conflicts with people around us, and the things we think we should be doing but aren't. Those are just a few examples; there are plenty more. And they are the ones we have to learn to "deal" with.

When I notice that knot forming in my shoulders, it's a trigger for me to step back and analyze the situation. My first step is to recognize that this is a bad stress situation and pinpoint exactly what it is that's got such a grip on me.

Once I know what it is, I have some options. First I assess whether it really deserves so much frenetic energy. I mean, is it worth losing sleep over, worth zapping my energy?

Then I choose between a couple of courses of action. I can distance myself from the situation for a while—to clear my head. I find exercise is a good outlet for me. You may find lifting weights, doing yoga, running a few miles, or kicking back with your iPod is the best thing for you. I look for an hour and inevitably some space to get between me and whatever's getting the better of me. Whatever your release is, use it.

The other option is dive right into figuring out how to take control of whatever is stressing you out. (If you choose the first option, this becomes step two.) Psychologists widely agree that control is the best remedy for stress. One control method comes from Allen Elkin, Ph.D., and director of the Stress Management and Counseling Center in New York. I love his approach. He says no matter what the challenge is, set it up in your mind and then alter the situation to make it less stressful. Do this in your mind's eye and rehearse your solution. This will give you the upper hand on whatever it is that's nagging you and you will have a better chance of determining how to get through it.

Another way to manage stressful situations is to turn a bad situation into a good one. For example, if you find your commute particularly stressful, take control by opting to make it at a less congested hour. If you can't do that, realign your mind and consider it found time in your day. Use it to your own benefit by listening to a book on CD, learning Italian, or catching up on the Podcasts you downloaded the day before. Or get a little work done by making phone calls (hands free, of course!) or if you don't have to have your hands on any kind of wheel, return emails wirelessly. There are tons of things you can do in a car or on a train besides letting the jerk in front of you get you upset.

Another mechanism for taking control is changing your mindset from "shoulds" into "coulds." For example, instead of feeling like you have to tackle the 50 emails in your inbox right away ("I should have them all answered by now! EEEK!"), take a breath and create a plan ("I could do 15 now, 15 after lunch, and 20 tonight when I get home."). "Should" puts pressure on you and emphasizes what you're not doing. "Could" puts you in control and makes the task manageable. You arrive at solutions. Once you have control of the situation it becomes a matter of executing a plan, not reacting to a stressor.

Of course, the best mechanism of all is balance. Finding a challenging and rewarding job, surrounding yourself with good people, saving enough dough to alleviate debt, taking care of your health, and making time for some fun (although, remember to pursue your dream and your job will be fun, too) are the keys.

Take time each day for yourself. If you don't make yourself happy, you probably won't make anyone else happy, and you'll have a harder time being productive. Make it a priority to keep balance in your life, and the little things are less likely to get you down.

## COMMON WAYS PEOPLE COMBAT STRESS

### SOME HEALTHIER THAN OTHERS . . .

Exercising

Playing music

Socializing

Yoga; meditation; alone time

Reading

Writing (creative, journal)

Partying

Watching TV

Eating too much or too little

Sleeping

# i'M BUYiNG MY FiRST CAR. HOW DO i GET A COOL CAR, iNSURANCE, LiCENSES, AND EVERYTHiNG ELSE THAT GOES ALONG WiTH iT AND NOT BREAK THE BANK OR MAKE A STUPiD MiSTAKE?

I know those hot rides can be tempting and once you get the car bug, it's hard to get over it. But before you get too far down the road, so to speak, you'll want to make sure you do a reality check. And that means, take a look at your budget. How much car you can afford involves more than just the price of the car. You have to think about a down payment, in cash, the monthly payment if you finance, insurance, tax, title, license and, of course, upkeep and fuel. Yes, when you buy a car, the purchase price is just the start of the costs!

So now that I've laid the reality out there, you're probably still thinking, "Yeah, so how do I get a cool car?" Here are some answers. First, consider getting a pre-owned version of that cool car. Look for one less than five years old with fewer than 50,000 miles. They say that the minute you drive a new car off a lot it loses a lot of its value, so let the first owner take that loss.

Next, try to find a car with payments that are no more than 10 percent of your monthly take-home pay. That will ensure that your car isn't a huge drain. At the same time, consider insurance. Research how much insurance will be for the car you want, in your state for a driver your age and gender with your driving record. Quotes are easy to get online. That will lend another dose of reality to what you can afford.

If you're still in the game, then go online and do your research so you're prepared to actually buy. Walk into a dealership knowing how much the dealer pays for the car (dealer invoice). That will help you when you negotiate the price. Never pay the sticker price; you should strive to pay some amount over invoice. A good source for this information is www.edmonds.com. There you can research any car—new or used—and get dealer invoice pricing information.

The big thing with cars is to know what you can afford, then don't over buy. It can be really hard, but know there are tons of choices out there and if you are patient and look around, the right car that looks cool and is fun to drive will appear.

# i'M YOUNG, i'M HEALTHY. DO i REALLY NEED MEDiCAL iNSURANCE?

I am absolutely alarmed every time I hear statistics about the number of people in the United States who don't have medical insurance. Last I heard the number was over 43 million. That's almost 15 percent of the population. I realize it's not a choice for most of these people. Coverage is expensive. That said, I'm happy to hear that insurers are starting to respond to the demand, particularly among young people—Blue Cross and Blue Shield of Colorado and California's Tonik Health Insurance, for example. They have three plans specifically for active young healthy people who need health insurance but hate forms and jargon. The plans are easy to understand and you can apply for them quickly right online at www.tonikplans.com. You can often be approved within minutes. So whether you are a "Thrill Seeker," a "Part-Time Daredevil," or a "Calculated Risk Taker," they have plans for you. Check it out.

Just how expensive is it to not have health insurance? A report from National Public Radio pegged prices as follows:

$7,000 per day for a hospital bed

$9,000 for a helicopter ride to the emergency room

$48,000 for an appendectomy

Do you see where I'm going with this? Not having health insurance is like betting your entire savings account for the next five or ten years on a roll of the dice. Your financial well-being is on the line. The last thing you want is to be forced into bankruptcy before you even have a bankroll to bust. Even worse, you don't want to sacrifice your health because you "can't afford to see a doctor" or took a job with poor health benefits.

And what if you took the job with no health coverage or poor health coverage? If that job is the one you need to get to where you want to be or you absolutely love it and have no intention of quitting, then you'll need to buy your own health insurance. Even if the job offers you limited coverage, you can supplement that with insurance that will make sure you are protected should health issues arise.

Yes, my friend, you really need medical insurance.

# HOW DO i BUY MEDICAL iNSURANCE? Earlier

I panned the Internet for its incredible ability to lure you in and drain your time. Here, I celebrate it as one of the quickest ways—outside of working for a company that provides you with medical insurance—to go about finding adequate medical coverage.

Health insurance options differ from state to state. One quick way to get a lay of the land is to do a Google search for "health insurance" plus the name of your home state. Thousands of results will come up. You should see some familiar company names (e.g., Blue Cross, Humana) and names of myriad insurance brokers. The brokers are essentially middlemen who connect potential buyers of health insurance with potential sellers.

Whether you click on the sites for the familiar companies or on those for the brokers, you will soon be presented with program descriptions and electronic applications. You can compare what's being offered and apply, all from the comforts of your living room or, should I say, laptop.

If you already know which doctor you prefer to see, another option is to call the doctor's office and ask for the names of the health insurance plans he or she accepts. This may help narrow your search considerably. I suggest you also ask the doctors (or their office staff) if they have any insight on which of the insurers seem more responsive to customers or are easier to work with.

Once you have identified the insurance providers you're interested in, determine what you can afford and make it a permanent entry in your budget. You'll have to balance the amount you can afford to pay on a monthly basis with the total amount in addition to premiums that you can manage to pay each year. Then fill out the applications and cross your fingers that you are accepted for a policy!

# HEALTH INSURANCE LINGO

## THESE ARE TERMS YOU NEED TO KNOW.

### CO-PAY

Fixed amount you will be charged every time you visit the doctor.

### DEDUCTIBLE

Amount out-of-pocket that you have to pay
before your provider starts kicking in.

### HMO

Acronym for "health maintenance organization," a health insurance plan
that is often less expensive with more limitations.

### OPEN ENROLLMENT

Time period during which employees can make changes to
employer-subsidized medical coverage.

### OUT-OF-POCKET MAXIMUM

Total amount that you will have to pay in a calendar year.

### PARTICIPATING PROVIDER

Term for health-care professionals who work with a particular
insurance provider or plan.

### PPO

Term for health-care professionals who work with a particular
insurance provider or plan.

### PRE-EXISTING CONDITION

A common limitation of coverage based on your injuries or illnesses
before getting coverage from a provider.

### PREMIUM

Monthly payment to keep an insurance policy in force.

### PRESCRIPTION BENEFIT

The amount the insurance company pays for prescription drugs.

# WHAT IF I DON'T HAVE A DOCTOR OR DENTIST? HOW DO I FIND GOOD ONES?

Well, one way not to find a medical professional is to go to the phone book. That should go without saying. The way you find a doctor or a dentist is the same way you find a good hair stylist—you ask around. But before you make that appointment for the root canal you need, check out the credentials of the doc. At the very least make sure he or she is part of your health insurance plan and in good standing. Go online and look up the records on your state's medical board. Does the dentist have any pending or past law-suits? Any disputes or actions? Did he or she get his degree from the best school in the nation or from a virtual dentistry correspondence course. This service can be free through your state's board of medicine, but other third party services may cost money.

Long story short, be a good consumer of medical services. A bad haircut will always grow back, but a dentist screwing up a root canal could cause problems for life.

# I JUST MOVED TO A NEW CITY. ANY SUGGESTIONS ON WHERE TO MEET PEOPLE?

When you move to a new city or state, you get to start with a clean slate and pursue a new direction. You get to reinvent yourself. The only downside is it's not always as easy to meet new people once you've finished school.

Likely the easiest way for you to make new friends will be through work. If you're a likable person, you'll naturally be-friend a few people on the job. Once they find out you're new to a city, I guarantee they'll go out of their way to invite you out socially. From there, it's up to you to be open to the invitations. If you prefer to keep your work life separate from your personal life (and many do), it becomes more a matter of spending time doing the activities you like to do. Check craigslist and community weeklies for activities and events in the area—and go participate! Join recreational sports leagues. Go to book signings and lectures on topics of interest. If you live in the sunbelt and live in an apartment, go hang out by the apartment pool. If you are religious, join a church. If you like to play fantasy sports, find a league in your town, apartment complex, or office. You can even join your school's local alumni association. Many get together to watch football or basketball games or do community service.

Your best bet is (here we go again) knowing yourself. Once you've got that down, it should be relatively easy to find people who share your interests.

## ANY iDEAS FOR REMEMBERiNG PEOPLES' NAMES?

If you're a poker player, you've heard a thing or two about "tells." In cards, these are signals (e.g., scratch of the hair, positioning of cards) that a player unconsciously gives that suggest something about his or her hand. Veteran players watch for tells in an effort to gain an advantage.

When you've forgotten someone's name, there's no tell more obvious than the extended "Heeeey!," the substitute "Hi buddy," or the many other variations that you've no doubt heard. It can be so embarrassing.

Alternatively, remembering a person's name unexpectedly can be incredibly powerful. It can make a great impression. It can help you win business, jobs, friends, and perhaps more important, respect.

If remembering names is a challenge for you, recognize it and take steps to fix it.

## HERE ARE SOME IDEAS

- Make the name visual. When you hear the name, literally picture yourself writing out the name on the person's forehead. Sounds crazy, but whatever canvas you choose, visualization gets your eyes working along with your ears. Authorities agree, the more senses you use, the better.

- Support your ears and eyes with your mouth. Repeat the name a few times immediately in conversation. The more you say the name, the more you train yourself to associate it with the face of your new acquaintance. And, if you are in a meeting and have paper in front of you, engage your sense of touch and write the name on the paper.

- Always ask for a business card and keep it in view either in your hand or on the conference table. Later, enter the person's name, title etc. in your address book or company data base and the place and date you met.

- Remember you can always ask a person to repeat his or her name. A simple, "I'm sorry, can you please tell me your name one more time" is better than faking it every time you see that person. And you can always ask a colleague in the know.

# IS IT A BAD IDEA TO DATE SOMEONE FROM WORK?

A 2005 survey from the career information company, TheVault.com, confirms that office romances happen. Almost 60 percent of the more than 600 survey participants said they have been involved in an office romance. That number seems surprisingly high, but the fact remains that more than half of people in the workplace get involved in one way or another.

Sometimes it's just a crush, sometimes it's a real fling. Other times the flingers get married. Regardless, if you're flirting with the idea of mixing business with pleasure, tread carefully.

Some companies have official policies about office romance. Some of those policies go so far as to suggest that violators risk losing their jobs and if there are nuptials, sometimes there are rules against spouses working for the same company.

And worst of all, what if your feelings aren't mutual? As you know, we also live in an incredibly litigious society. Official policy or not, nothing could kill a reference faster than a sexual harassment suit initiated by a person who wants nothing to do with you.

Many people will say that office romance is only a problem when quality of work becomes compromised. I appreciate the opinion, but all things considered, I encourage you to steer clear of dating co-workers—particularly when you're just starting out on the job.

It's hard enough to separate your work life and your personal life as it is. When the main person sharing your personal life sits three cubicles away, you can pretty much forget about trying to keep the two separated. Differences of opinion or competition (you are vying for the same account or promotion) at work become more personal. It can put co-workers in an uncomfortable position (especially after a break-up). I won't even get into the hazards of dating a boss or a subordinate. And there's no way to avoid questions about your productivity if you're working together.

Then there's pillow talk about expense reports, salaries, weekly meetings, and tyrannical bosses. No, office romance just isn't a good idea. Best not go there. Instead, try to keep the relationship a friendship if at all possible. Eventually one of you will move on and you can strike up the heavy stuff later.

# I'M COMING TO THE REALIZATION THAT I CAN'T AFFORD TO LIVE ON MY OWN, SO I'M THINKING ABOUT MOVING BACK IN WITH MY PARENTS. ANY POINTERS?

This can happen. A lot of people find themselves living at home again and for some it is no big deal; for others, it's nothing short of traumatic. Regardless of which way you feel, you will want to set limits on your return to the nest. Life can get pretty comfortable, especially if you are enjoying all the perks: someone to do your laundry, make your meals, and free room and board. So probably the bigger question is how do I make my return home a temporary set up?

## HERE ARE SOME THOUGHTS

- Voice out loud to yourself and your family that this is a temporary situation. Sometimes saying something out loud makes it real. You'll be more apt to make your return home truly temporary if you tell yourself and everyone involved, "This is just for six months."

- Set up a financial plan for regaining your independence. This is so important. Before you return home, determine how long it will take you to get back out on your own. Put a savings plan together, figure out a way to pay off your debts. Map it all out by month—your savings, your debt reduction, and your expenses—and you'll know exactly how long you'll be gracing Mom and Dad with your presence.

- Live by house rules and pitch in. Don't expect to return home and pick up right where you left off. Your parents may see you as an adult now and expect you to act like one. That means offering to pitch in with cleaning, cooking, yard work, etc. Plus, you're invading someone else's space; make a point to be respectful of others' lives.

- Realize, you may have to give up some of your freedoms. Those all night parties and all night house guests might have to go on hiatus when you're at home. What you do in your own house is your business; what you do in your family's house is theirs.

- Pitch in on expenses – either in the form of a modest rent or buying some groceries. This will go a long way to remaining an adult in your childhood enclave. It's too easy to slip back to being a kid when you return home.

Take nothing for granted—when you are able to strike out on your own again, make sure you thank your family for their help. I don't care how cool your parents are, few of them in their 40s, 50s, or older expect their grown kids to be living with them. They are doing it because they love you and want to help. That deserves a lot of thank you's.

# HOW DO i FiND A MENTOR? When asked who they turn to for mentoring in and after college, my co-authors had fairly consistent answers. The majority turn to their parents. Former coaches, former managers, professors, aunts, and uncles were other popular choices. I guess the good news is they have people to turn to. I got mixed reviews when I asked how often the guidance was helpful. Perhaps you can relate?

There's no question about the value of having a mentor in life—someone whose advice and guidance helps you through the good times and the bad. A mentor is a person who has walked the walk before, who has made the mistakes, and who has had the wins. The true value of a mentor isn't just advice; it's experience that can help you progress faster and make smarter moves. Great mentors can even inspire.

Your mentor will most likely not be a person wearing a formal "mentor" tag. Rather mentors are most likely informal helpers in your life. A mentor can be a person in your profession, like a boss, or someone you know personally, like a family friend. You may have a different mentor for each aspect of your life. Some mentor relationships are strictly business, where you get together to go over issues you're facing. Others are simply friendships you might have with a person, usually older than you, who you learn from without really trying. Many of my co-authors had mentors to help them make decisions about whether they should get advanced degrees, whether they should look for new jobs, determine the certifications they need to get the jobs they want, and to even just figure out their lives.

In college my mentor was my math teacher. Not only was he gifted at teaching but he was highly accomplished. More than that, he always made himself available to students, and he sincerely cared. He was patient and so obviously loved his profession that I thought, "I want to be like that." The part I haven't told you was that Dr. Irving O. Bentsen was blind. He lost his sight at age 14. He had a huge impact on my life, and many of the lessons I'm conveying in this book are ones he helped me see.

A mentor should be someone you admire, trust, and respect; someone you can speak openly with about challenges, both personal and professional. A good mentor won't simply validate your direction, but he or she will help you approach crucial decision making with a realistic perspective—one that's different from yours. A good mentor is a person who also wants to guide others and cares about people.

Unfortunately, good mentors can be hard to come by. One approach to finding mentors is to literally seek them out. Alumni networks and professional organizations often have formal mentoring programs linking the more experienced members with the less experienced members. Alternatively, you can seek out referrals from family members, friends, or colleagues, to people who may be able to lend you a voice of experience. Yes, there are online places like MySpace.com, LinkedIn.com and others where you may find an online mentor, but we live in a three-dimensional world and nothing replaces the face to face with a real person.

More often than not, you just sort of stumble upon your mentor. I realize this doesn't give you a lot to go on, but keep your eyes and ears open and don't be afraid to ask someone older and more experienced in life for advice. Maybe ask them to review your résumé. Maybe ask for input on a decision you have to make. Sometimes a small opening like that can open the door to a great relationship. You typically have to make the first move. Mentor relationships evolve; seldom does anyone say, "Hey, can you be my mentor?" It just happens when you learn from a person or several people.

Regardless of who it is, you have to start somewhere. Like any other meaningful relationship, a mentor relationship is one you have to build.

# RESOURCES

## THESE ARE SUGGESTED RESOURCES FROM BOTH 20-SOMETHINGS AND THE AUTHOR.

For a more complete list refer to Additional Resources (see page 228).

www.mindtools.com
www.about.com/health
www.edmunds.com
www.tonikhealth.com

# 9

# MY ELEVEN "MUST KNOWS"

**EVERY CHAPTER IN THIS BOOK STARTED**

with a real life story from someone I met
while working on this book. The issues
were so similar no matter who I talked
with, that the subjects this book should
cover became self evident. And hidden
behind all the questions and concerns,
the hopes and opportunity, was the un-
asked question, "What kind of person
should I be?"

There are few times in your life when you get to invent or reinvent yourself. Entering college was one of them. Entering the real world and your first real job is another one. This chapter puts forth a few opinions I like to call "Must Knows" that I think you should consider when you are reinventing yourself. What you do with them is up to you.

## CALL ME STUPID. Here's a piece of advice you didn't ask for: Think twice before you take a construction job working for your girlfriend's father.

Call me stupid, but I took a summer job working on bridge construction under the direction of my girlfriend's dad. I knew the job would be hard work, but it was cool because I got to work a jackhammer. What I didn't expect was to learn a lesson I'd carry with me all my life. It started on the first day when this tough construction worker took me aside and said, "Hey college boy, I just want you to know, you'll get no special treatment here. You see those guys over there. If they don't show up for work, or they don't put in a good day's work, I send them down the line. I'll do the same to you."

As tough as it was, and there were many days when I was so tired I wondered what possessed me to take this job, I look back on that summer and know it was worth it. Not only did my boss demonstrate that being a "college boy" didn't entitle me to any special treatment, he taught me an important lesson about integrity and discipline.

Now you have arrived at the proverbial life lessons of this book. I'm certainly not trying to place myself on the same high pedestal that I have since put my construction boss on, but my intent is to put these "Must Knows" out there where you can benefit from them if you choose to. You may relate to them immediately, or their significance may sneak up on you when you least expect it, a kind of "ah ha" moment we all have sometimes. That's how most of them came to me.

Paying attention to these "Must Knows" will not only make everything in the book easier to swallow, but they will also form the foundations for the rest of your life. It's the stuff you didn't know you needed to work on. Call it the wisdom of experience, or even the "if-I-only-knew-then-what-I-know-now" stuff. Of course, I had to learn much of this the hard way. You may have to, too. But when you're in the midst of that tough lesson, you may recall this book and say "ah ha!"

> "When I was 18, I was amazed at how ignorant my father was.
> When I was 21, I was impressed at how much
> the old man had learned in three short years."
>
> **MARK TWAIN**

# MUST KNOW #1: PACE YOURSELF.

If you are running a marathon, you don't start out in an all-out sprint. You pace yourself, whether your goal is to win, to better your last time, or simply to complete the race. The same goes for work. It's fine to get to the office earlier than required, contribute long hours and weekends, and take work home with you. But ensure you maintain that delicate balance. If you find yourself in a job that is eating up your personal time, step back—something isn't right.

There will be times in your life when you need to make extraordinary commitments, but they should have definable beginnings and ends, just like finals week in college. You may join a company with lofty goals that require you to dedicate most of your waking hours to achieving this success. But if you find yourself in that same high gear after years of dedication with the big pay off nowhere in sight, it's probably time to rethink what you're doing and look for something else.

Remember, your goal is to succeed in your career, in your family, and in your personal life, and even to exceed your own initial expectations. Surprising yourself is great, but keep a pace that doesn't burn you out and make you a one-dimensional, all-work kind of person.

It's like being on a one-hour leisurely bike ride, only to look at your watch and find more than two hours have gone by. You get caught up in the moment, enjoying the view or the exhilaration or the opportunity to sort through some thoughts. The ride becomes therapeutic, making your body and mind feel good. You maintain a comfortable pace and find you are actually capable of going farther and faster than you expected.

The same concept applies to work. You will exceed your ambitions if you set a pace that can be maintained—not too slow that you get complacent, and not too fast that you become overwhelmed, impatient, stressed, and burned out. It's pacing that will leave room for your own personal needs and the needs of your family.

## MUST KNOW #2: PRACTICE. PRACTICE. PRACTICE. Golf legend Jack Nicklaus, when he was at the peak of his game, was once asked by a reporter what skills he

practiced after a great round. He said he practiced the shots
he hit poorly in the round and other shots he didn't hit at all.
Imagine, the number one golfer in the world celebrating a great
round with . . . practice. Vijay Singh, who battles with Tiger
Woods for best golfer in the world, does the same thing today.
In fact, even after he wins more than a million dollars in a tour-
nament, he is notorious for staying on the driving range until
it is so dark he can't see his ball. It's that kind of discipline and
drive that makes the talented great.

The same applies to you. Know what you are good at, what
shots you routinely hit well and which ones you never seem to
make. Then practice the latter. Maybe its public speaking; if so,
find a speech coach who can help you, read books, join Toast-
masters. There are lots of ways for you to improve. Then practice the shots you didn't hit; in other words, diversify your skills.
If you're in a job that is very narrow in its scope, maybe branch
out in your next position and do something out of your comfort
zone and commit to learning it. It never hurts to be well rounded.
And if you commit to constantly practicing and challenging
yourself, not only will you become the best you possible, your
life will be infinitely more exciting and rewarding.

## MUST KNOW #3: TiME iS MONEY. I know
this sounds like a small thing, but punctuality matters in the
workplace and in life, plain and simple. Think of it this way.
If an employer pays four people an average of $50 per hour,
and one individual is late to a meeting while the others are
left waiting, that's at least $200 of pay wasted. If it were your
company, would you want to pay employees to sit around and
shoot the breeze?

## THERE ARE MANY CONSEQUENCES WHEN PEOPLE ARE LATE

- Productivity declines.
- Time, money, and resources are wasted.
- Colleagues are distracted.
- Other appointments become delayed.
- You jeopardize your credibility.

My guess is you know people who always keep you waiting. Regardless of how punctual you are for meetings with these people, you still sit and wait. Remember how you feel when your time is wasted. That's how people feel when they have to wait on you.

When you plan your commute, plan to be early. That way when something unsuspected occurs, like a traffic jam, you have a buffer. If you know you are going to be late for a meeting, call ahead so people can make the decision to wait or start without you. Respect other peoples' time, and they will respect yours.

# MUST KNOW #4: CHARACTER iS DEFiNiNG. There are certain personal characteristics that withstand the test of time. In today's society, people worship movie stars, athletes, and even some international political figures. But only when we delve into their personal lives—how they live day to day—do we see what these individuals are really about, and it's not always so praise worthy.

Defining your own character isn't just about defining you on the surface, like a model on a magazine cover. It means delving into your daily life, how you handle problems, what you think of others, how you treat people. It's easy to be of great character when things are rosy, but how are you when times are tough? They say everyone has integrity until it's tested.

Brace yourself, you will encounter difficult and challenging times. How will you handle setbacks and roadblocks? The manner in which you treat others and how quickly you obtain resolve will help define your character.

Character is not something that is bred or inherited. It is the by-product of good habits. Live your life every day committed to doing the right thing, and when those difficult times arise, you will be so used to doing the right thing that you won't be able to do anything but that.

I don't claim to be a highly spiritual or religious person, but I truly believe in some form of karma. I believe that what you do to others will ultimately come back to you. If you take a person of solid character and add strong values, the result is a high integrity person. And I don't know anyone who wouldn't want to be thought of that way.

## MUST KNOW #5: DOiNG WHAT'S RiGHT CAN BE HARD. We live in a world of options. Usually the right path and the wrong path are pretty obvious. For example, let's say you're a sales rep. With every potential customer you visit, you'll assess whether your product or service will help this person, whether the sale will help your company, or whether it will

simply put money in your pocket. Having any one of these without the other two is clearly not right. Are you going to line your pockets at the expense of the customer and the company? Are you going to benefit the company at the expense of the customer? And are you simply going to give a product away to a customer at the expense of the company being able to stay afloat?

That's an obvious example, but how do you really know right from not right? Here's the test: When there's no need to conceal any part of the facts and you have a clear conscious—that voice of ethics in your head—then the action is usually right. Notice the word "and," it's not "or." The reason is simple: too often it is easy for us to justify doing the wrong thing by feeling entitled. You know the self talk: "Well, it's only a $55 dinner added to my expense report. And we did talk a little about business. Besides, the company owes me at least that for all the extra hours I put in. They can afford it. And on my last trip, I didn't eat breakfast one morning, so I saved them money there."

Sometimes taking the right path is incredibly hard to do. But when you put a premium on doing the right thing, the results will come back to you. Those around you will recognize it. You will create longer-term relationships, and you'll sleep better at night.

## MUST KNOW #6: TRUST iS EVERYTHiNG. Building

trust takes time, but once you earn it, it's a bond that's tough to break. Life is about relationships and relationships are built on trust. No matter if we are talking about your personal life or your work life, trust is a true key to peace and happiness. Take a marriage. If your spouse thinks that every time you are late coming home that you're having an affair, life is going to be pretty miserable. And on the job, if your customers don't trust that you are giving them your best price, it's going to be difficult to get any more business from them. Trust is the very foundation of any lasting relationship. And what kind of dividends does it pay? Sometimes money, but most reliably it leads to the richness of life, made up of things like respect, admiration, and, most importantly, friendship and love.

# MUST KNOW #7: THERE ARE DEGREES OF FRIENDSHIP.
We all enjoy having a diversity of friendships, but one thing you will realize as your career and your personal life progress is that not all friendships will survive the test of time. Pay close attention to the friends who are there for the fun times but disappear when you need support.

I have always been close with my brother, John. He has been my sounding board for so many issues in my life. One time in particular, when I was struggling with some of my perceived close friendships, he offered up a friendship litmus test. He told me to ask myself these three questions:

## FRIENDSHIP LITMUS TEST

1. Would you trust this person with your money or worldly possessions?

2. Would you trust this person to look after someone you love when you won't be around for an extended period of time?

3. Can you trust this person with your life? Would this person be able to make life or death decisions about you or someone you love in a medical emergency?

Asking these three questions will make it easier to categorize the depth of your relationships. If the answers aren't clear, you may want to reset your expectations of this friendship. It doesn't mean you need to tell the friend to take a hike. It simply helps you put things in perspective.

## MUST KNOW #8: SAY WHAT YOU'LL DO, AND DO WHAT YOU SAY.

This may seem obvious, but it's actually a rule that many people forget. It's frustrating when someone makes a commitment and then fails to deliver. In an ultra-competitive business environment, you can excuse people for over-committing themselves once in a while, provided they made a sincere effort or events beyond their control prevented them from getting the job done.

There are too many people, however, who provide lip service and commit to actions they have no intention of following through on. If this is your MO (modus operandi), you'll want to change it right away because it will limit you in every aspect of your life.

## MUST KNOW #9: PASSiON YiELDS SUCCESS.

Pour your heart into it and strive to find a career that you can be as passionate about as you are about your hobbies. Otherwise, you may not recognize your full potential, or if you do, it will happen grudgingly without much enjoyment.

John C. Maxwell's *The 21 Indispensable Qualities of a Leader* offers a very succinct lesson on passion and leadership. In the book, he describes a dispassionate young man casually approaching the Greek philosopher Socrates and saying, "Oh great Socrates, I come to you for knowledge."

Socrates leads the man to the sea and proceeds to dunk his head underwater and hold it there for 30 seconds. When he lets the young man up for air, Socrates asks him to repeat what he wanted. "Knowledge, oh great one."

Socrates dunks his head again. After repeated dunking and questioning, the young man finally gasps, "Air, I want air!" "Good," says Socrates. "Now, when you want knowledge as much as you want air, you shall have it."

Don't let yourself be pushed to the brink of drowning to realize your passion. Passion comes from within. Find a field that you genuinely love, where you will actually enjoy learning everything you can—and it won't be work—then commit yourself to excellence. Your success and passion for your chosen field will become infectious.

# MUST KNOW #10: WHEN YOU GIVE YOU GET IN RETURN. Giving will yield rewards, but they may
not be immediate. Sometimes the benefits go beyond our generation and are a legacy to others. Giving could be as simple as opening a door for someone, donating blood, volunteering your time, or giving money to a worthy cause. When need arises, are you someone that will go the extra mile to help?

Probably the most sincere gift an individual can give is anonymous help to others, without the expectation of anything in return. It's not only the wealthy who can contribute, but also people who volunteer their time, intellect, and ingenuity in resolving world problems.

You will encounter hardship in your life—perhaps personally, perhaps professionally, perhaps both. Financial hardship is among the most common. It may be your own, your friends', your relatives' or your colleagues'. Quite often this strife comes from being out of work, but more often it's a combination of poor financial planning and bad spending habits. While loaning money to help people get back on their feet certainly can be noble, I've learned that we have much more to offer than money.

## HERE ARE A FEW IDEAS

- Help with a job search or reconstructing their résumé.
- Help by networking with industry or personal contacts.
- Review business plans.
- Write letters of recommendation.
- Serve as a reference.
- Act as a sounding board for ideas or opportunities.

Granted, you may not be in a position to do any of this right now, but keep it in mind as you achieve your own success. And look for ways you can help people in other areas of your life. You will realize far greater satisfaction and recognize far better returns by helping others achieve their dreams than you ever could by simply buying them through a problem that they never learned to fix.

## MUST KNOW #11: YOU LIVE WITH THE CHOICES YOU MAKE.

The last "Must Know" is that the choices you make will impact your life and your lifestyle. You will have to live with them and every choice brings with it consequences, both good and bad.

The choices you make affect how you balance your life, and my co-authors were concerned about balance. If you can figure out how to balance an inspiring career and a lifestyle you'll enjoy, you will be better off than 99 percent of the world's population. It's really challenging to find the dream job that is fun, pays well, and provides you the freedom and sense of accomplishment everyone wants. Find all four of those elements—enjoyment, money, freedom, and accomplishment—in your life, then balance them and that may very well be the definition of happiness.

Choose a high-profile career path in corporate America, for example, and it likely comes with the burden of stressful work and hours that are way too long. The choice compromises your freedom but probably delivers on the financial side. Other lower-paying jobs still may be hard work, but they may deliver a real sense of accomplishment. White water rafting guides are great examples. They take people on life-changing adventures and often make a huge difference in helping people overcome the fears and obstacles we all put in front of ourselves. Guides get months off at a time and get to spend their days in beautiful wilderness. But the pay, well, that can be low.

Your choices will impact balance. And frustration comes when you choose a career path and expect it to be something it's not. No person choosing the path of corporate executive should expect to have summers off. If you expect that kind of free time and that is critical to life balance, then there will be a problem. Just as in our society and unfortunately so, a person who chooses to be a wilderness adventurer shouldn't expect to be able to afford a BMW on a guide's salary. If that person does, he or she is in for some major disappointments.

How much is enough for the lifestyle you want to lead? What is a want versus a need? Figure it out early. That way you'll be less likely to find yourself torn between working for a paycheck and working at something that brings you satisfaction and enjoyment throughout your life.

## KEEPiNG TRACK OF BALANCE

Keep track of your life. Every month write down what's going on in your career, your family life, and your personal life. Think in terms of your enjoyment, freedom, money, and accomplishment. Try your best to keep in balance by having something to report in all three areas of your life. If you find yourself reporting all career highlights and few personal or family ones, then adjust the next month. Balance is all about conscious effort and follow through.

Your 20s can be the most challenging time of your adulthood. Or it can be one of the most exciting, a time that sets you up for the rest of your life. It's up to you. Many of my co-authors were fearful of the future, so much so that they were frozen in place and frozen in time. They were in essence doing exactly what they were so afraid they would be doing in 30 years—waking up every morning hating their lives. You don't have to live that way, now or later, but recognize that if you do, it is your choice. And you will continue to make choices, moment by moment, to achieve whatever you want to achieve, make the money you want to make, and be free to do what you want to do. And when you add it all up, you go to bed thankful for the day you just had and you wake up looking forward to the day that is to come. You begin to realize that this is what "happy" is—having enough longing to keep life interesting, but enough enjoyment and contentment to keep you feeling safe.

Yes, it is the thrill of accomplishment, the resource of money, and the promise of freedom that lead to an enjoyable life. A truly happy life. A life that takes you from surviving to thriving in your 20s, in your 30s, 40s, 50s, and beyond.

Here's to a long and happy life and to no more ramen.

# ADDITIONAL RESOURCES

**HERE IS A LISTING OF ADDITIONAL RESOURCES.
FOR MORE, VISIT WWW.NoMoreRamenOnline.com.**

## FINDING INFORMATION/NEWS

Google.com

NYTimes.com

CNN.com

MSN.com

ESPN.com

current.tv

latimes.com

washingtonpost.com

mondotimes.com

Amazon.com

ivillage.com

## MEETING OTHER PEOPLE/NETWORKING

anywho.com

thefacebook.com

Itsjustlunch.com

MySpace.com

match.com

AmericanSingles.com

eHarmony.com

FriendFinder.com

Friendster.com

ge-dating.com (Great Expectations)

LoveCompass.com

PerfectMatch.com

Yahoo.com

linkedin.com

## CAREER EXPLORATION

www.career.fsu.edu/ccis/matchmajor/matchmenu.html
http://web.stlawu.edu/career/exploration
http://www.uhs.berkeley.edu/Students/CareerLibrary/Links
http://career.missouri.edu/students/explore

## RÉSUMÉ WRITING

collegegrad.com

Resumeedge.com

jobweb.com

### BOOKS

*Résumé Magic: Trade Secrets of a Professional Résumé Writer,* Susan Britton Whitcomb, Indianapolis: JIST Works, Inc, 2003. Comprehensive and effective, displays a plethora of résumé options, formatting tips, strategy and emphasizing accomplishments.

*Best Resumes for College Students and New Grads,* Kursmark, Louise M, Indianapolis: JIST Works, Inc, 2002. Focuses on limited work experience, new college grads targeting entry-level employment.

## JOB SEARCH

Simplyhired.com

Monster.com

craigslist.com

careerbuilder.com

jobfinder.com

dice.com (specializes in high tech)

ebullpen.com (finding the perfect job)

hotjobs.com

jobfinder.com

jobhuntersbible.com

salary.com

jobkabob.com

# iNDEX

# ABOUT THE AUTHOR

**NICHOLAS ARETAKIS** is a 40-something who's been a 20-something and remembers all too well how challenging and confusing finding your place in the real world can be. He also is a 40-something who has helped hundreds of 20-somethings find happiness in their lives. Is he a Ph.D., psychologist, career counselor, or sociologist? No, he's a guy who conquered his 20s, became a millionaire by 30, and helped countless others get their start in life all along the way. Through it all, he chronicled what worked, what didn't, and discovered that balance is everything. But beyond personal experience, Aretakis interviewed hundreds of people in their 20s to get at the heart of today's issues. Aretakis is a graduate of Columbia University, Hobart and William Smith College and an executive with a leading technology firm. He continues to council people just starting their careers, face-to-face and through **www.NoMoreRamenOnline.com**.

## ADDITIONAL COPIES & INFO

FOR ADDITIONAL COPIES, ORDER THIS
BOOK FROM YOUR FAVORITE BOOKSTORE
OR AMAZON.COM, OR CONTACT US AT:

Next Stage Press, LLC
24950 N. 107th Place
Scottsdale AZ 85255
480.993.3740

FOR MORE LINKS AND INFORMATION,
AS WELL AS THE *NO MORE RAMEN*
BLOG AND TOOLBOX, VISIT
www.NoMoreRamenOnline.com.